The Art of the Book

Illustration and Design, 1650 to Present

Edited by

Joan Stack

Associate Curator, Museum of Art and Archaeology

Prefaces by

Alex W. Barker

Director, Museum of Art and Archaeology

&

James A. Cogswell

Director, University Libraries

With contributions by:

Erin Walcek Averett *(EWA)*

Sarah Carter *(SC)*

Kelli Bruce Hansen *(KBH)*

Jessica Kelty *(JK)*

Holly Robbins *(HR)*

Joan Stack *(JS)*

Susan Wood *(SW)*

Sponsored by
Museum of Art and Archaeology and University Libraries
University of Missouri-Columbia

Published in conjunction with the exhibition *The Art of the Book: Illustration and Design, 1650 to Present*, which ran from September 16 through December 24, 2006, at the Museum of Art and Archaeology, University of Missouri-Columbia, Columbia, Missouri.

This catalogue was made possible by funds from the University Libraries, the Museum of Art and Archaeology and The State Historical Society of Missouri's Richard S. Brownlee Fund.

The Museum of Art and Archaeology would like expressly to thank Special Collections, Ellis Library at the University of Missouri-Columbia and The State Historical Society of Missouri at the University of Missouri-Columbia, for the manuscripts and books lent for the exhibition. Various objects in the exhibition were also lent by private collectors, some of whom wish to remain anonymous.

Exhibition Curator and Organizer: Joan Stack

Publication Designer and Supervisor: Bruce T. Cox

Museum Director: Alex W. Barker

Director of University Libraries: James A. Cogswell

University Archivist, Head of the Special Collections, Archives and Rare Book Divisions: Michael E. Holland

Cover: James Caldwall (British, 1739–1819)
Indian Reed (detail), 1804, from *The Temple of Flora* by Dr. Robert Thornton
Color engraving with aquatint and stippling on paper
Museum of Art and Archaeology, University of Missouri-Columbia
Gift of Mr. Rowland H. Smith in memory of Jane Froman (89.72)

Frontispiece: Aubrey Vincent Beardsley (British 1872–1898)
How Guenever Made Her a Nun (detail), 1909
From *Le Morte d'Arthur* by Sir Thomas Mallory
Line block print
Special Collections, Ellis Library, University of Missouri-Columbia

Preface illustration: Jean-Pierre Simon (British, ca. 1750–ca. 1825)
After Henry Füseli (Swiss, 1741–1825)
The Enchanted Island before the Cell of Prospero—Prospero, Miranda, Caliban and Ariel, Act I, Scene II of The Tempest (detail), 1797
From *A Collection of Prints from Pictures for the Purpose of Illustrating the Dramatic Works of Shakespeare by the Artists of Great Britain,* published by John and Josiah Boydell, London, 1803 (preface dated 1805)
Stipple and line engraving
Museum of Art and Archaeology, University of Missouri-Columbia (87.128)

Endpiece: Henri Matisse (French, 1869–1954)
Aeolus, Cave of the Winds, 1935
Illustration for *Ulysses* by James Joyce
Soft ground etching
Museum of Art and Archaeology
University of Missouri-Columbia
Gift of Museum Associates (92.79.2)

ISBN 0-910501-38-6

All photographs were provided by the office staff of the Museum of Art and Archaeology, University Libraries and The State Historical Society of Missouri.

CONTENTS

PREFACE I

Alex W. Barker
Director

Museum of Art and Archaeology
University of Missouri-Columbia

Books permeate our lives so thoroughly that it is easy to forget how arbitrary a convention they are, one among many possible ways of creating contexts for the graphical presentation of information. Scholars debate what characteristics make something a book and the boundaries of where books *sensu stricto* end and other forms of graphical representation (scrolls, for example, or electronic files) begin. But while "bookness" remains a debated concept, none would dispute the central role books play in the communication and perpetuation of both human knowledge and a broader understanding of the human condition.

Books, Rufus Choate once said, are the only immortality. And some of the works included here certainly qualify as immortal. Newton's *Principia*, for example, revolutionized scientific understandings of physics, astronomy and mathematics. Illustrated by geometric diagrams, the *Principia* was an attempt to deal objectively with universal phenomena using both subjective language (in the case of the *Principia*, Latin) and culturally-specific, arbitrary representational conventions. Joyce's *Ulysses*, illustrated by Matisse, certainly qualifies as another immortal work. Matisse references both Joyce's masterwork and the parallel episodes from the *Odyssey* that are reflected and refracted in Joyce's narrative. Similarly, Charlotte Brontë's marvelous "play" not only constitutes a manuscript book in its own right but also recapitulates printed books in both conception and design. In each of these cases, illustration and design not only support the book's written content but also add new layers of meaning and complexity. The Ediciones Vigía publication of Nancy Morejón's *Ana Mendieta* is an excellent example of this theme. Hand-constructed with a variety of found materials, the book was created and designed to celebrate Mendieta's artistic works; the media encapsulates and enhances the message.

A previous exhibition explored the art of the book from its beginnings to 1650. In this new exhibition, *The Art of the Book: Illustration and Design, 1650 to Present* and its accompanying catalogue, Associate Curator Joan Stack turned her attention to the past 350 years, a period when books became mass-produced commodities. As both exhibition and catalogue demonstrate, however, the art of the book remained vital and vibrant despite, and perhaps in part because of, these technological and economic changes. Aesthetics of book design, book illustration and an *objets d'art* book approach continue to inform, influence and inflect the idea of the book in exciting ways. Indeed, one reason books resist an easy definition is that they represent a constantly changing and evolving concept. Artists continue to push the edges of the concept. They explore and explode our views of what books represent and how they represent meaning to us, and create new kinds of books, new ways to see books and new ways for books to touch our lives. This exhibition celebrates that continuing evolution.

Associate Curator Joan Stack organized this exhibition and coordinated the compilation of this catalogue. She worked closely with staff members of the University of Missouri Libraries' Special Collections Archives and Rare Books Division, including Kelli Bruce Hansen and University Archivist and SCARAB Division Head Michael Holland. James Cogswell, director of libraries, provided constant support and encouragement, and without his support neither this exhibition nor this catalogue could have been completed. Stack, Hansen, Erin Walcek Averett, Sarah Carter, Jessica Kelty, Holly Robbins and Susan Wood contributed content to this catalogue; MAA Interim Assistant Director Bruce Cox designed and coordinated the publication of this catalogue. Images used in this catalogue were provided by The State Historical Society of Missouri, Assistant Director of the University of Missouri Library Systems Office, Kurt Kopp, Registrar of the Museum of Art and Archaeology, Jeff Wilcox and Rob Hill of the *Illuminations* magazine. All of the Museum staff members contributed to the success of this exhibition, but particular recognition should be given to Bruce Cox, Jeff Wilcox, Interim Director Jane Biers, Chief Preparator Barb Smith, Assistant Preparator Larry Stebbing and student assistants Jennifer Haile and Josh Jacomb for their successful mounting of this exhibition. Biers, Carter, Hansen, Holland, Kelty, Kathy Lowery, Christine Montgomery, Wilcox and Wood reviewed this catalogue in various stages of production, and we are grateful for their thoughtful comments. Andrell Bower provided her expertise and comments in the final editing of the catalogue.

Support for this exhibition catalogue came from the University of Missouri-Columbia Libraries, the Museum of Art and Archaeology, The State Historical Society of Missouri's Richard S. Brownlee Fund, and private benefactors of the Library Society. In addition to the collections of the University of Missouri System Libraries and the Museum of Art and Archaeology, several institutions and individuals generously provided books and illustrations. We are particularly grateful to The State Historical Society of Missouri, Dr. Juanamaria Cordones Cook and to other donors who have chosen to remain anonymous. We gratefully acknowledge their support.

Finally, I wish to thank my colleagues at the University of Missouri for sharing their knowledge and expertise—and their books—to make *The Art of the Book: Illustration and Design, 1650 to Present* a reality.

PREFACE II

James A. Cogswell
Director of Libraries

University Libraries
University of Missouri-Columbia

The enduring legacy of one of humanity's greatest technological achievements—print on paper—is lovingly celebrated in this exhibition and catalogue, *The Art of the Book: Illustration and Design, 1650 to Present*. Both the exhibition and the pages of this catalogue elegantly guide the reader through an important period of refinement and maturity in the history of graphic communication. Through beautiful and intriguing examples of printing and graphic arts, they trace the evolution of recorded knowledge and aesthetic achievement from monotype codices and copperplate illustrations to modern fine-press book editions and fine art prints.

Expanding and continuing her 2003 exhibition, *The Art of the Book: Manuscripts and Early Printing 1000–1650*, Joan Stack, associate curator for European and American art at the University of Missouri-Columbia, has again juxtaposed the rich collections of the Museum of Art and Archaeology with the extensive yet largely unheralded materials in the MU Libraries' Special Collections Archives and Rare Books Division. The books selected from the University Libraries' collections are among the most important works of printers, book designers, artists, binders and publishers.

Library materials featured in the exhibition include a pair of manuscript novels written in a minuscule hand by Charlotte Brontë in 1833. The exhibition also includes two seminal works of modern microscopy and microbiology: Robert Hooke's 1667 edition of *Micrographia; or Some Physiological Descriptions of Minute Bodies Made by Magnifying Glasses*, printed by James Allestry for the Royal Society of London, and Antoni van Leeuwenhoek's first Latin edition of *Opera Omnia* from 1719. The University Libraries also contributed a 1935 Limited Editions Club printing of James Joyce's *Ulysses* that was illustrated and signed by Henri Matisse.

The rare books collection of the University of Missouri-Columbia is the product of many dedicated individuals, including private collectors, rare-books librarians and distinguished scholars. Late faculty members Dr. Hellmut Lehmann-Haupt and Dr. Homer Thomas were especially critical to the development of the collection. Margaret Howell who died this year, deserves recognition as a principal architect of the collection during her time as head of the special collections division. Throughout her distinguished career, she selected, organized, promoted and preserved large parts of the collection for future scholars and students. Additional gifts from the Friends of the University of Missouri Libraries and many generous private donors have continued to build an internationally recognized cultural treasure.

Many individuals provided critical support for this extensive effort. Along with Stack, other staff members of the Museum of Art and Archaeology rendered invaluable assistance in the project, including Dr. Alex Barker, Dr. Jane Biers, Bruce Cox, Jeffrey Wilcox, Larry Stebbing, Erin Walcek Averett, Sarah Carter, Jessica Kelty, Holly Robbins and Susan Wood. Kelli Bruce Hansen of the Special Collections Archives and Rare Books Division and Michael Holland, University archivist and head of the SCARAB Division, coordinated the loan of items to the Museum of Art and Archaeology. A final word of appreciation must be given to Kurt Kopp, assistant director of the University of Missouri Library Systems Office, who provided the serial collection's digital images used in this catalogue.

In addition to the Museum of Art and Archaeology and the University Libraries, The State Historical Society of Missouri's Richard S. Brownlee Fund and private benefactors of the University of Missouri-Columbia Library Society supported the printing of this catalogue. In addition to being a splendid example of the art of the book, the catalogue is a testament to what can be accomplished through public and private partnerships that are dedicated to advancing learning and culture.

INTRODUCTION

Joan Stack
Associate Curator

*Museum of Art and Archaeology
University of Missouri-Columbia*

The *Art of the Book: Illustration and Design, 1650 to Present* is a sequel to *The Art of the Book: Manuscripts and Early Printing 1000 to 1650*, the highly successful 2003 exhibition at the University of Missouri's Museum of Art and Archaeology of manuscripts and early printing. The current exhibition and catalogue explore aesthetic aspects of book production between the seventeenth and twenty-first centuries. Included are books from the University of Missouri Libraries' Special Collections and leaves and books from the Museum of Art and Archaeology, The State Historical Society of Missouri and the collections of several private lenders.

The exhibition and catalogue are divided into three sections. The first section examines the empirical world and includes books and illustrations related to science, nature, geography and architecture. The second section is devoted to literature and includes illustrated novels, plays and poetry books. The final section focuses on books dating from the 1930s to the present. All the works come from Missouri collections, and while the selection is by no means comprehensive, the objects and artwork document important cultural, social and economic changes that have affected book design over the course of 350 years.

Artists helped instigate these changes. Illustrations animate, materialize and organize verbal concepts, and the sizes and physical appearances of books affect their interpretation. Beginning in the eighteenth century, some artists worked with publishers to create giant luxury books with large striking illustrations that rivaled panel paintings in their beauty and monumentality. Such books were often experienced in communal settings. Their size allowed groups of people to leaf through their pages and enjoy their illustrations collectively. In the libraries of wealthy individuals and scholarly institutions, the shared aesthetic experience of these large texts and their illustrations often educated and entertained.

Not all aesthetic innovations in book design focused on large format texts. Many artists exploited the fact that reading is usually an intimate and solitary experience. Sometimes this experience is primarily aesthetic. A reader or viewer can flip through an illustrated text and understand it chiefly as a series of images. Moreover, since most books consist of a series of pages bound between stiff covers, their pages can be read and viewed in or out of sequence. This format provided artists with a communicative platform that was experienced over time and often (but not always) in conjunction with the written word.

An illustrated book taps into the cultural *esprit* of its era in unique and powerful ways. This exhibition includes many examples of books that were illustrated and designed by some of the finest European and American artists of the last 350 years. Since the Middle Ages, books with pictures have been popular, yet illustrated volumes have always been more expensive to manufacture than text-only editions. In this catalogue, readers will see examples of the inventive ways that publishers and artists produced, promoted and distributed their illustrated books between the seventeenth and twenty-first centuries.

Artists were sometimes intimately involved in the publishing business. They distributed their own books and solicited buyers with "book tours," lectures and catalogues. As publicity became increasingly important, artists and publishers regularly advertised their books with prospectuses describing and promoting upcoming editions. Many also sent advance copies of early chapters and illustrations to journalists and respected intellectuals. If a book received favorable evaluations, the written opinions of these reviewers were often incorporated into prospectuses. They functioned much like the excerpts from critical reviews that appear on today's book jackets and advertisements do.

In the eighteenth and nineteenth centuries, many expensive illustrated books were published by subscription. They were issued in parts, sometimes called "fascicles" or "numbers." Each part contained a section of text or a selection of illustrated plates or both. When all the parts were received, subscribers usually paid to bind the books. This publication process could take many years to complete, which allowed the cost of the project to be spread out over time and reduced the need for a large initial capital outlay on the part of the artists, editors or publishers. This system also permitted subscribers of moderate means to buy expensive books in installments.

Technical innovations in printmaking also affected the publishing business. By the seventeenth century, the intaglio technique of copperplate engraving had replaced the woodcut as the preferred method for making book illustrations. To make an engraving, printmakers incised lines into plates, which were inked and wiped. The ink remained in the grooves, and the plates were printed with roller presses that forced the pigment from the incised lines onto the paper. This technique allowed for large editions of 2000 or more copies to be printed before the plates began to deteriorate. Many engravings were spectacularly beautiful, and the process allowed for the reproduction of drawings on a grand scale. Making plates was often a collaborative process. Professional engravers were frequently employed to copy artists' original paintings and drawings onto copper. Other modes of intaglio printing on copper, such as etching, mezzotint and aquatint, allowed printmakers to create images with more tonal qualities than traditional line engravings had. The delicacy of these plates, however, usually limited the number of good impressions that could be pulled from a single matrix to between 100 and 300. Larger editions could be produced by techniques that combined etching and engraving.

By the nineteenth century, industrialization facilitated the manufacture of books by cutting the costs of printing, papermaking, coloring and binding. New technical innovations such as steel plate engraving, wood engraving and lithography made possible the production of large editions of inexpensive books with quality illustrations. Steel plates were more durable than copperplates and deteriorated more slowly. Likewise, the blocks used to make wood engravings were extremely hard-wearing because they were carved from the fibrous end grains of very hard woods (traditional woodcuts were carved along the grain). Finally, the introduction of lithography, a planographic technique in which images are printed from greasy crayon or touche drawings on limestone, revolutionized the industry. Invented by the German publisher Aloys Senefelder in 1796, this process made it possible for printmakers to create tonal drawings on stones that resembled chalk or watercolor sketches. Litho stones could be used to print thousands of impressions, and by the second half of the nineteenth century, printmakers had perfected color lithography (sometimes called chromolithography), a process that used multiple stones (and later litho plates) to mimic the chromatic qualities of paintings.

While many illustrators made the monochromatic nature of their works a virtue, color attracted consumers and was often added by hand in the seventeenth, eighteenth and nineteenth centuries. Most colorists used transparent watercolors to tint engravings, etchings and lithographs. The painters were usually given a model print colored by the master printmaker to copy, and sometimes the process was carried out by a team of colorists, each of whom painted a section of the engraving, etching or lithograph. In the eighteenth and nineteenth centuries, some printmakers experimented with color printing techniques such as the *à la poupée* method of inking copperplates with multiple colors or the process of inking several plates with a different color to create a single image. However, these techniques could be almost as time-consuming and expensive as hand coloring.

In the late nineteenth century, printers perfected the photogravure process, line block printing, half-tone block printing and other photomechanical techniques that allowed publishers to reproduce drawings, paintings and photographs cheaply and efficiently. These photomechanical reproductions replaced original prints as the most common type of book illustrations in the twentieth century. However, some artists reacted against this trend, and books published by old-fashioned printing methods became popular among an elite group of consumers. Many of these books were released in special limited editions that commanded high prices and were primarily bought by collectors and libraries. Today, as computerization and digital imaging are revolutionizing the publishing world, some artists continue to rebel against the impersonal aspects of modern technology and create new, hand-printed and hand-made books. Many of these contemporary artists' creations are designed for a new kind of audience that appreciates the materiality of the books and experiences the texts as sculptural aesthetic objects.

Note to the Reader

The entries in this catalogue were written by the curatorial staff of the Museum of Art and Archaeology and the staff of Special Collections at the University of Missouri-Columbia's Ellis library. The authors are listed on the title page, and their initials appear at the end of their entries. Several graduate students and undergraduate interns from the Department of Art History and Archaeology at MU contributed to the catalogue, which could not have been completed without their diligent work.

For the sake of the reader, notations have been kept to a minimum and are indicated parenthetically. Each entry includes only a selected list of the most relevant references. For more complete bibliographies, readers should consult these sources. A general bibliography that includes all the literature cited in the entries and uncited general reference works can be found at the end of the volume.

The Empirical World
Nature, Architecture and Geography

Joan Stack
Associate Curator

*Museum of Art and Archaeology
University of Missouri-Columbia*

Some of the most spectacularly illustrated books are non fiction studies of architecture, geography and natural history. From an early date, authors realized that words could not completely and scientifically describe their empirical observations. Pictures and diagrams complemented texts and sometimes superseded them as communicative tools.

While the selection is not comprehensive, the books and leaves in this section of the catalogue provide viewers with a sample of architecture, travel and nature books produced in the seventeenth, eighteenth and nineteenth centuries. The monumental size of many of these volumes may surprise modern viewers who are accustomed to the more modest dimensions of illustrated books that sit on today's coffee tables. As this exhibition demonstrates, many of these enormous books were eventually torn apart and their painting-sized illustrations sold as independent artworks.

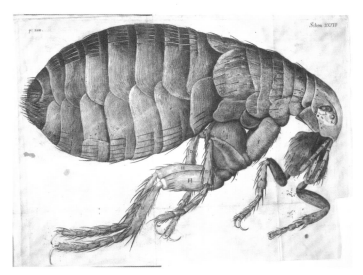

CATALOGUE 1
*Robert Hooke
(British, 1635–1703)*
***Micrographia; or, Some
Physiological Descriptions
of Minute Bodies Made by
Magnifying Glasses***
*(Page no. 210, **Flea,** pictured)
Printed text with engravings
Special Collections, Ellis Library
University of Missouri-Columbia*

MEASUREMENTS
30 x 21 centimeters (cover)

Robert Hooke was a scientific polymath whose discoveries, inventions and accomplishments ranged from physics to biology to architecture. He served as an assistant to the English physicist Robert Boyle in his early career and was instrumental in the discovery and mathematical expression of Boyle's Law, which deals with the volume and pressure of gases at a constant temperature. In 1660 Hooke went on to discover the principle of compression and stretching, now called Hooke's Law, becoming famous for his work with microscopy. He began to perform experiments with a microscope in the early 1660s and went on to make the first recorded observations about many of the microscopic details of daily life.

Hooke's findings were published in the book *Micrographia* in 1665 and were accompanied by plates engraved after his own detailed drawings. This landmark work was the first investigation of many fundamental biological discoveries. It included the first description and representation of a cell, a name Hooke coined, as well as the first investigations of the life cycles of insects and the structures of hair, mold and feathers.

With the publication of the *Micrographia*, the learned public turned its attention for the first time to the smallest components of existence. The seventeenth-century diarist Samuel Pepys, for example, recorded that he stayed up until two o'clock in the morning pouring over "the most ingenious book that I ever read in my life," and the ideas it presented resonated deeply in the popular and literary imagination of the time (Andrade, 141). According to the review in the *Philosophical Transactions* of the Royal Society,

> . . . *a new visible world is discovered to us by this means, and the Earth shews quite a new thing to us, so that in every little particle of its matter, we may now behold almost as great a variety of creatures, as we were able to reckon up in the whole Universe it self* (*Philosophical Transactions*, 27).

Micrographia's illustrations allowed readers to visualize in vivid detail the microscopic structures and creatures that, unbeknownst to them, had always existed alongside them in their everyday lives. The foldout plate of the flea (pictured above) became the most famous and iconic image associated with the work. In it, the viewer observes minute details of the insect's anatomy blown up to many times life-size. Although the engravings were made after Hooke's own drawings, it is thought that some of the plates may have been produced with the assistance of the architect Christopher Wren, one of Hooke's close associates.

The *Micrographia* became an immediate bestseller, which afforded Hooke both scientific and commercial success. The book went through two early editions, one that predated the 1666 London fire and one in 1667. The Missouri copy is from the second edition and has the James Allestry imprint. The original plates were reused for the second printing except for plate 5, which was re-engraved in reverse.

REFERENCES
"An Account of the Micrographia, or the Physiological Description of Minute Bodies, made by Magnifying Glasses." *Philosophical Transactions* 1, no. 2 (1665): 27–32.

Andrade, E. N. da C. "Robert Hooke, F. R. S. (1635–1703)." *Notes and Records of the Royal Society of London* 15 (July 1960): 137–145.

Carter, John, and Percy H. Muir. *Printing and the Mind of Man*. Munich: K. Pressler, 1983.

Dibner, Bern. *Heralds of Science as Represented by Two Hundred Epochal Books Selected from the Burndy Library*. Norwalk, Conn.: Burndy Library, 1955.

Keynes, Geoffrey. *A Bibliography of Dr. Robert Hooke*. Oxford: Clarendon Press, 1960.

CATALOGUE 2
Antoni van Leeuwenhoek
(Dutch, 1632–1723)
Opera Omnia, *1719*
Printed text with engravings
*(Page no. 275, **Winged Insect**,*
pictured)
Special Collections, Ellis Library
University of Missouri-Columbia

MEASUREMENTS
21 x 17 centimeters (cover)

REFERENCES
Dobell, Clifford. *Anthony van Leeuwenhoek and His "Little Animals."* New York: Harcourt, 1932.

Ford, Brian J. *Single Lens: The Story of the Simple Microscope.* New York: Harper and Row, 1985.

Palm, L. C. "Leeuwenhoek and Other Dutch Correspondents of the Royal Society." *Notes and Records of the Royal Society of London* 43, no. 2 (July 1989): 191–207.

Parker, G. H. "Anthony Van Leeuwenhoek and His Microscopes." *Scientific Monthly* 37, no. 5 (Nov. 1933): 434–441.

Schierbeek, Abraham. *Measuring the Invisible World: The Life and Works of Antoni van Leeuwenhoek.* New York: Abelard-Schumann, 1959.

Stein, John Bethune. "On the Trail of Van Leeuwenhoek." *Scientific Monthly* 32, no. 2 (Feb. 1931): 116–134.

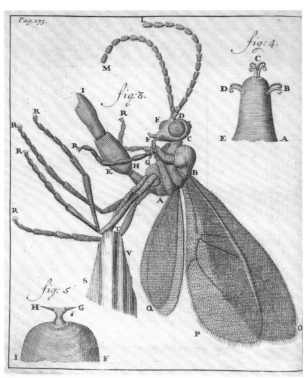

Although now regarded as the father of microbiology, Antoni van Leeuwenhoek had virtually no scientific training. Born in Delft, he was trained as a draper and probably became acquainted with optical instruments in the form of the magnifying glasses that cloth merchants used to judge the quality and texture of their wares. It is likely that Robert Hooke's *Micrographia* of 1666 (see Cat. 1) inspired him to make his own experiments with optics, and by 1668 he had developed a method of making lenses by blowing and grinding glass spheres. Although Leeuwenhoek worked with simple microscopes, his most advanced lenses achieved a magnification power almost ten times as strong as that of Hooke's compound microscope.

Leeuwenhoek used his new technology to build upon Hooke's work and discovered various microorganisms, which he termed *animalcules*. He first published his work in 1673 by writing to the Dutch scientist Reinier de Graaf, who forwarded his letter to the Royal Society of London. His observations on mold, the stingers of bees and the louse were published in the Society's *Philosophical Transactions* later that year.

Leeuwenhoek's career included the discoveries of several types of bacteria, microscopic animals such as nematodes and rotifera, red blood cells and spermatozoa. Being among the first to observe circulation in capillaries, Leeuwenhoek also described the motion of the blood in veins. He was invited to join the Royal Society of London as a full Fellow in 1680, a significant honor for a foreign correspondent with no official scientific credentials. Although he never left Delft, he corresponded regularly with Hooke and other members of the Society, and his findings were often published in the Society's *Philosophical Transactions*. Leeuwenhoek continued sending letters about his discoveries to the Royal Society until his death in 1723 at the age of 90.

Leeuwenhoek never learned any language other than Dutch, and he never published a monographic work. All of his letters to the Royal Society had to be translated into English for publication, and publishers began to gather them into collections within his lifetime. The four-volume *Opera Omnia*, published in 1719, translates the letters into Latin for a wider scientific audience. It also includes engravings, such as the anatomical study of a winged insect pictured above, that illustrate Leeuwenhoek's observations.

KBH

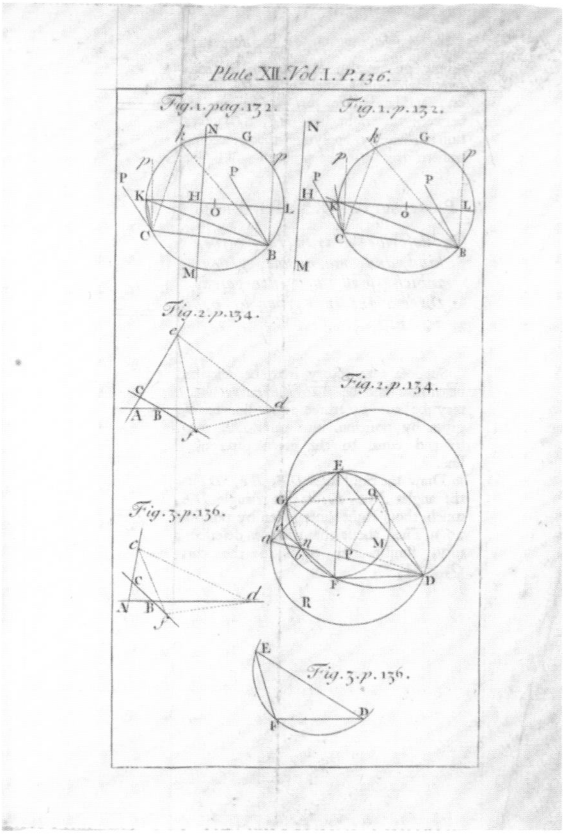

Sir Issac Newton first published his *Philosophiae naturalis principia mathematica* in 1687. One of the landmarks of scientific thought, the book explains the physics, or "mathematical principles," behind various phenomena in the natural world. The *Principia* was the first explication of differential calculus as well as the new science of dynamics. Other concepts discussed in the book are mass, centripetal force, gravity and inertia.

The book's publication came about by chance. In 1684 the astronomer Edmond Halley visited Newton and recounted a discussion he had with Robert Hooke and Christopher Wren about the nature of planetary orbits that are produced by inverse-square central force. Newton had calculated the answer years before but was unable to find the mathematical proof, which later took the form of a nine-page treatise titled *De Motu* (On Motion). At Halley's urging, Newton published the work. He found that once he got started writing about his theories it was hard to stop. Newton continued to revise and elaborate on the principles in *De Motu*, and over the next two years he organized his writings into the massive *Principia*. The Royal Society licensed its publication in 1686.

The *Principia* was originally published in Latin and divided into three books: "The Motion of Bodies" (books 1 and 2) and "The System of the World" (book 3). In the first two books, Newton laid out his laws of motion concerning the relationships between force, mass and direction. Fusing physics and astronomy into a science, the third part applies these laws to the motions of the heavenly bodies. This science later came to be called celestial mechanics. Throughout the book, engraved geometric diagrams such as the one pictured above illustrate Newton's theories and observations.

At the time of its publication, the *Principia* revolutionized scientific and mathematical thought and attained for Newton great prominence within the scientific world. Even so, the book was not immediately accepted by the scientific community. Part of the reluctance to embrace Newton's ideas resulted from academic intransigence, and Newton's exclusive use of Latin and the small print run of the first edition also meant that his ideas could only gain footing among certain sympathetic members of the intellectual elite. Both Newton's own esoteric style and the difficulty of his topic also contributed to the slow acceptance of his work.

Newton edited two subsequent editions of the *Principia* during his lifetime, one in 1713 and another in 1726. Responding to criticisms from other scientists, he drastically revised some sections, added mathematical proofs and discarded several of his theories. The entire *Principia* did not appear in English translation until after Newton's death. The copy in Special Collections at Ellis Library is from the first English edition, translated by Andrew Motte and published in London in 1729.

KBH

CATALOGUE 3
Sir Isaac Newton
(British, 1642–1727)
The mathematical principles of natural philosophy
Translated into English by Andrew Motte, 1729
Printed text with engravings
(Plate no. 12, from Vol 1, pictured)
Special Collections, Ellis Library
University of Missouri-Columbia

MEASUREMENTS
19.5 x 13 centimeters (cover)

REFERENCES
Fara, Patricia. *Newton: The Making of Genius.* New York: Columbia University Press, 2002.

Gray, George J. *A bibliography of the works of Sir Isaac Newton, together with a list of books illustrating his works; with notes by George J. Gray.* Cambridge: Bowes and Bowes, 1907.

Newton, Sir Isaac. *The Principia mathematical principles of natural philosophy; a new translation by I. Bernard Cohen and Anne Whitman assisted by Julia Budenz; preceded by A guide to Newton's Principia by I. Bernard Cohen.* Berkeley, Calif.: University of California Press, ca. 1999.

Review of *Philosophiae naturalis principia mathematica. Philosophical Transactions of the Royal Society* 16 (1686): 297.

CATALOGUE 4
Jacques Philippe Le Bas
(French, 1707–1763)
After Julien David Le Roy
(French, 1724–1803)
and Louis-Joseph Le Lorrain
(French, 1715–1759)
Vue des Ruines d'un Temple de
Corinthe (View of the Ruins of
a Temple at Corinth), *1758*
*From **Les ruines des plus beaux***
monuments de la Grèce
(The Ruins of the Most
Beautiful Monuments of Greece)
Engraving
Museum of Art and Archaeology
University of Missouri-Columbia
Gift of Museum Associates in
honor of Dr. Jane C. Biers
2006.8

MEASUREMENTS
39.2 x 56 centimeters (sheet)

REFERENCES
Harris, Eileen, and Nicholas
Savage. "Stuart and Revett,"
in *British Architectural Books*
and Writers (1556–1785).
Cambridge: Cambridge
University Press, 1990,
439–450.

Le Roy, Julien-David. *The*
Ruins of the Most Beautiful
Monuments of Greece.
"Introduction" by Robin
Middleton. Translated by
David Britt. Los Angeles:
Getty Publications, 2004.

Wiebenson, Dora. *Sources*
of Greek Revival Architecture.
London: A. Zwemmer, 1969.

Julien David Le Roy was the son of Julien Le Roy, a celebrated clockmaker for the French king Louis XV. The young Julien studied architecture and became an early advocate of the classical style in France. Financed by his father, he made an expedition to Greece between 1754 and 1755 to record, sketch and measure Grecian ruins. When the young architect returned to Paris, he arranged (in association with the antiquarian Anne-Claude-Philippe de Tubières, comte de Caylus) to publish a descriptive account of his journey with views, elevations, plans and details of the ruins he encountered during his travels. He also wrote discourses on architectural theory and history to accompany the text.

Le Roy sought to capitalize on the burgeoning interest in classical Greece that was emerging in the 1750s. He was aware of the proposals of Englishmen James Stuart and Nicholas Revett to produce the multivolume book on the antiquities of Athens (printed proposals had been circulating from 1752 onward, but the first volume of Stuart and Revett's *The Antiquities of Athens* did not appear until 1762). Upon his return to Paris in 1755, the enterprising Le Roy speedily contracted to have his Grecian sketches copied and engraved, and in 1758 (four years before the appearance of Stuart and Revett's book) *The Ruins of the Most Beautiful Monuments of Greece* was published.

Le Roy's copiously illustrated book articulated the aesthetic sensibilities of European Grecophiles and influenced the thinking of later eighteenth-century and nineteenth-century neoclassical artists and architects. Although illustrated architectural books focusing on the antiquities of Rome had been popular in Europe since the Renaissance, little literary or aesthetic attention had been devoted to the architecture of ancient Greece until the eighteenth century. While there are precedents for *The Ruins of the Most Beautiful Monuments of Greece* (Richard Pococke published measured drawings of the Parthenon in 1743), Le Roy's book was the first study of classical Greek architecture to have an international impact on public taste.

The *View of the Ruins of a Temple at Corinth* was plate 25 in the first edition of Le Roy's book. It pictures the remains of one of Greece's oldest temples, the Temple of Apollo at Corinth, which dates to the middle of the sixth century B.C.E. Thirty-eight Doric columns originally supported this peristyle structure, but Le Roy pictures only fourteen erect pillars (seven columns stand today; some were removed by a Turkish owner in the nineteenth century and some others now lie on the ground).

Like all the views in *The Ruins of the Most Beautiful Monuments of Greece*, the *View of the Ruins of a Temple at Corinth* was based on an original sketch of the monument made by Le Roy at the site. Le Roy's drawings were apparently very crude and were copied and reinterpreted by Louis-Joseph Le Lorrain, a painter known for his elegiac landscapes. Lorrain's drawings were then turned over to Jacques Philippe Le Bas, one of France's finest engravers and a specialist in landscape prints. Many of the resulting engravings depict oblique-angle views of ancient architecture overgrown with vegetation and silhouetted against dramatic skies. Providing the viewer with a sense of scale, small figures often stand near the ruined buildings. In *View of the Ruins of a Temple at Corinth*, the figures also establish a "modern" political and social context for the image. The men in the foreground wear Turkish dress, and we see a minaret to the right of the temple in the background.

JS

Le Bas Sculp.

Vue des Ruines d'un Temple de Corinthe.

Le Roy Arch.t del. en Grece.

CATALOGUE 5
Giovanni Battista Piranesi
(Italian, 1720–1778)
Opere di Giovanni Battista
Piranesi, Francesco Piranesi
e d'altri
(The Works of Giovanni
Battista Piranesi, Francesco
Piranesi and Others)
*(Table 20 from Vol. 7, **Various***
Roman Ionic Capitals
Compared with Greek
***Examples**, pictured)*
1835–1837
Printed text, etching and engraving
Special Collections, Ellis Library
University of Missouri-Columbia

MEASUREMENTS
88 x 67.5 centimeters (cover)

Although Italian artist Giovanni Battista Piranesi studied architecture and engineering in his native city of Venice, he is best known for the magnificent architectural prints he executed in his adopted home of Rome. The artist advertised his engravings and etchings in catalogues and was intimately involved in the marketing of his work. Although he sometimes obtained financial support from publishers and occasionally received subsidies from the pope and other patrons, much of his profit came from his entrepreneurial ventures. He made his catalogues available to dealers who bought both individual impressions and complete bound sets to sell to their diverse clients. He also sold prints in his own shops on the Roman Via del Corso and Strada Felice (now Via Sistina), both fashionable commercial thoroughfares. The large etchings and engravings were especially popular among tourists, who bought them as souvenirs and later displayed them in folio volumes in their libraries. The Venetian Pope Clement the XIII (1758–1769) exploited Piranesi's popularity by periodically purchasing bound sets of the prints to give to visiting dignitaries.

The print pictured at left originally appeared in Piranesi's 1761 book, *Della magnificenza ed architettura de' romani* (*On the Magnificence and Architecture of the Romans*). This collection of architectural images celebrated the innovation of Roman architects and rebutted the argument that their creations were derived from Greek precedents. Piranesi was particularly annoyed by the negative assessment of Roman architecture found in Julien-David Le Roy's *Les ruines des plus beaux monuments de la Grèce*, published in Paris in 1758 (a plate from which is also illustrated in this catalogue [see Cat. 4]).

Piranesi introduced *On the Magnificence and Architecture of the Romans* with essays in Latin and Italian that argued that the architecture of Rome developed from that of the Etruscans, not the Greeks, and that it was superior to Grecian architecture. This argument was made pictorially in the engravings that followed. Many of the prints included visual and verbal quotations from Le Roy's *The Ruins of the Most Beautiful Monuments of Greece*. For example, in the plate, *Various Roman Ionic capitals compared with Greek examples,* Piranesi included copies of Le Roy's representations of the fifth-century Athenian Erechtheum and a quote from the French writer's text that reads in translation, "[t]he Ionic capitals one sees in Rome seem poor and defective." This quote is surrounded by examples of magnificent Roman Ionic capitals. Below the text, we see the famous Roman landmark the "bocca della verità" ("mouth of truth"). According to legend, if an untruthful person placed his or her hand in the mouth of this ancient maskeron, it would bite off the appendage. Piranesi seems to suggest that his images, like the "mouth of truth," reveal falsehood—in this case the falsehood of Le Roy's text.

This print was one of many images reprinted in a twenty-seven volume edition of Piranesi's complete work titled *Opere di Giovanni Battista Piranesi, Francesco Piranesi e d'altri* (*The Works of Giovanni Battista Piranesi, Francesco Piranesi and Others*), published in Paris between 1835 and 1837. These mammoth volumes reproduced 940 etchings and engravings by Giovanni Battista Piranesi, 269 prints by his son Francesco and 231 works by other artists. The collection was published by the firm of Firmin Didot, which acquired the original plates after the death of Piranesi's son in 1810. In 1839, the firm sold the plates to Pope Gregory XVI, who placed them in their present home, a Roman institute for the graphic arts now known as the Calcografia dell' Istituto Nazionale per Grafica.

JS

REFERENCES
Ficacci, Luigi. *Piranesi: The Complete Etchings*. London: Taschen, 2000.

Scott, Jonathan. *Piranesi*. New York: St. Martin's Press, 1975.

Wilton-Ely, John. *The Mind and Art of Giovanni Battista Piranesi*. London: Thames and Hudson, 1978.

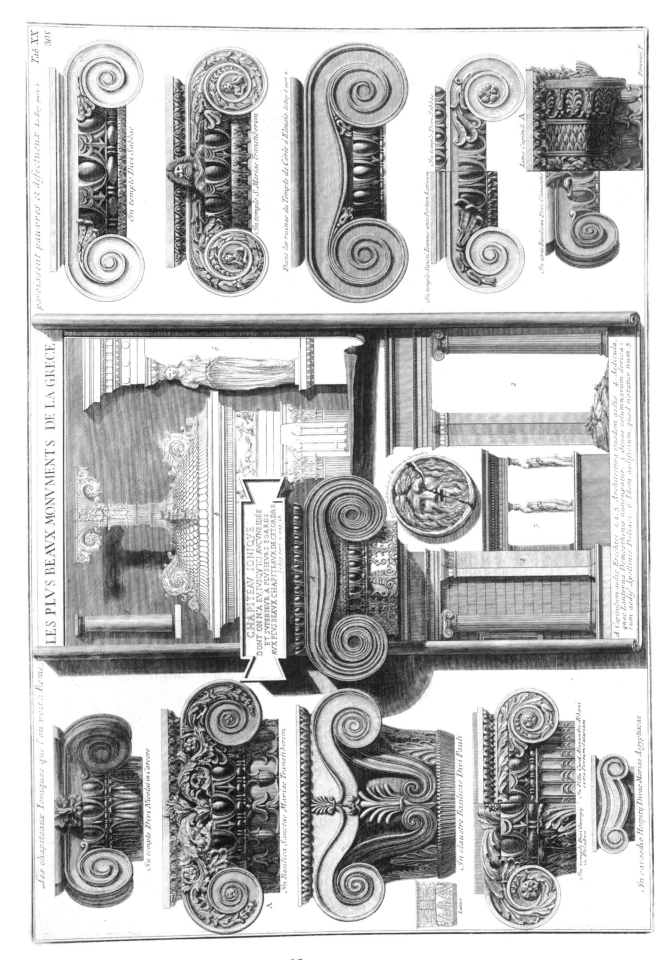

CATALOGUE 6
James Caldwall
(British, 1739–1819)
After Peter Henderson
(British, active ca. 1799, died 1829)
The Nodding Renealmia, *1801*
From Robert Thornton's **The**
Temple of Flora, *1799–1807*
Color engraving with aquatint
and stippling
Museum of Art and Archaeology
University of Missouri-Columbia
Gift of Mr. Rowland H. Smith
In memory of Jane Froman
89.71

MEASUREMENTS
55.3 x 45.3 centimeters (sheet)

REFERENCES
Buchanan, Handasyde.
Thornton's Temple of Flora.
London: George Rainbird
Limited, 1951.

Desmond, Ray. *Great Natural
History Books and their
Creators.* London: British
Library; New Castle and
Delaware: Oak Knoll Press,
2003.

Sitwell, Sacheverell,
and Wilfrid Blunt. *Great
Flower Books, 1700-1900: A
Bibliographic Record of Two
Centuries of Finely-Illustrated
Flower Books.* London: Collins,
1956.

Thornton, Robert. *The Temple
of Flora.* London: 1799–1804.
Reprint, Boston: New York
Graphic Society, 1981.

*T*he Temple of Flora, a magnificent and monumental flower book, was commissioned by Robert Thornton (ca. 1768–1837) in 1799 and completed in 1807. Originally destined for the priesthood, Thornton studied medicine at Cambridge University, where he developed an interest in botany. After inheriting a significant fortune following the deaths of his father, mother and brother, Thornton embarked on the extravagant production of *The Temple of Flora*. The book paid homage to Carolus von Linnaeus (1707–1778), who created a classification system for different plant species in his *Systema Naturae* (first published in 1735).

During the seventeenth, eighteenth and nineteenth centuries, colonization and travel encouraged public interest in classification systems of nature and led to the publication in Europe and America of grand botanical texts such as William Curtis' *Botanical Magazine* and Georg Dionysius' *Trew's Plantae Selectae*. These works were distributed in parts to subscribers, whose payments helped pay for production costs. Subscribers, who were often friends and associates of the authors, shared the cost of production by paying an initial deposit and then remitting the remaining amount upon completion of each section of the book. The buyers would accumulate the parts, or fascicles, and would eventually bind the sections into folios. Since subscribers were often essential to the success of books, authors and publishers frequently offered fascicles at reduced rates or deferred payment. Thornton decided to issue *The Temple of Flora* in twelve to fourteen fascicles at a cost of one guinea each. Each part included two plates and associated letterpress pages.

The book was expensive, and Thornton sold only around 700 copies. Six went to members of the royal family; nine to 'foreign kings and potentates', and seventy-four went to English nobility. Of the remaining, Thornton sold 294 to the Gentry, 266 to medical gentlemen, thirty-seven to florists and fourteen to "Public bodies." Unfortunately, the project failed to attract enough subscribers to pay for its costly production. In an attempt to cover these costs, Thornton convinced the British Parliament in 1811 to pass an act that allowed him to hold a public lottery. The first prize was the group of original paintings from which the plates for *The Temple of Flora* were made. The idea to raise money by holding a public lottery was inspired by the lottery of John Boydell, who sold the paintings of his Shakespeare Gallery to finance the publication of his mammoth book of engravings made after these paintings (a print from Boydell's book appears in Cat. 23). Thornton blamed his lack of sales on increased taxation and economic constraints that resulted from the French Revolutionary War. The lack of sales, however, was not caused solely by economic factors. Thornton produced his luxurious book during a time when the demand for flower books was waning and zoology texts, mostly in the form of ornithological books, were becoming more popular. Ultimately, *The Temple of Flora* did not cater to the tastes of consumers. The cost of production combined with the lack of sales exhausted Robert Thornton's inheritance, and when the author died in 1837, his family was nearly destitute. Today, the book and its plates are sought after by museums, libraries and collectors, and *The Temple of Flora* is considered one of the greatest flower books ever produced.

The Nodding Renealmia is plate 13 in the book. James Caldwall's aquatint illustration is based on a painting by Peter Henderson. According to Thornton's text, the plant is native to China and Japan and can grow to a height of nearly twenty feet. Sir Joseph Banks introduced the nodding renealmia to the West in around 1792. The plant blooms in May and is known for its pink sweetly scented flowers. Thornton was impressed by the flower's inflorescence (opening in stages). The plant's name is derived from one of its stages of bloom during which the flower stalk gradually curls over, or nods.

SC

The Nodding Renealmia

CATALOGUE 7
James Caldwall
(British, 1739–1819)
After Peter Henderson
(British, active ca. 1799,
died 1829)
Indian Reed, *1804*
From Robert Thornton's **The**
Temple of Flora, *1799–1807*
Color engraving with aquatint
and stippling
Museum of Art and Archaeology
University of Missouri-Columbia
Gift of Mr. Rowland H. Smith in
memory of Jane Froman
89.72

MEASUREMENTS
55 x 45.5 centimeters (sheet)

s one of history's most renowned flower books, *The Temple of Flora* contains thirty-one plates that were produced by a variety of techniques, including aquatint, stipple engraving and line engraving. To produce the prints, several printmakers copied flower paintings by a variety of artists who etched and engraved the images onto copperplates. Tonal effects were achieved by using the stipple technique, a way of representing values as a series of tiny dots and flecks, and the aquatint process, a method of creating tones with powdered resin that is applied to the plate and etched so that the final product has the appearance of a wash drawing. Color impressions were created using the *à la poupée* technique, in which each color is applied to the plate by hand before the printing of each proof. Finally, the prints were finished by hand colorists, which made every copy of the book unique.

Conventionally, flower books isolate the plants from their natural context and picture them against plain white or black backgrounds. However, in this book the exquisite flowers are situated within natural settings. Art historian Charlotte Klonk argues that the images combine the picturesque, the beautiful and the sublime and relates the botanical illustrations to the landscapes of the Romantic painters of the period. She goes on to say that the backgrounds function like those in eighteenth- and nineteenth-century portrait paintings. Instead of serving a scientific function, these backgrounds reflect the plants' perceived "characters" in Romantic, monumental images.

The *Indian Reed* is plate 30 in *The Temple of Flora.* The plant's scientific name is *Canna indica*, and it is a well-known garden flower used for formal bedding. The plant's blossoms come in a variety of colors, including yellow, orange, pink or red, and it can grow up to six inches tall. Because the Indian Reed originated in tropical climates, it is placed in an exotic setting in the illustration. The river in the background is probably the Ganges in India, and the pagoda adds an eastern touch to the picture. This plate is unique in the series because Thornton objected to Caldwell's depiction of the flower's spikes. In the final stages of production, Thornton had his hand colorists add a petal to each flower and a long pointed bud at the top. This is the only illustration in the collection that Thornton took such drastic measures to modify.

SC

REFERENCES
Desmond, Ray. *Great Natural History Books and their Creators*. London: British Library, 2003.

Klonk, Charlotte. *Science and the Perception of Nature: British Landscape Art in the Late Eighteenth and Early Nineteenth Centuries*. New Haven; London: Yale University Press, 1996.

Sitwell, Sacheverell and Wilfrid Blunt. *Great Flower Books, 1700-1900: A Bibliographic Record of Two Centuries of Finely-Illustrated Flower Books*. London: Collins, 1956.

Thornton, Robert. *The Temple of Flora*. London: 1799–1804. Reprint, Boston: New York Graphic Society, 1981.

Indian Reed

CATALOGUE 8
Robert Havell
(British, 1793–1878)
After John James Audubon
(American, 1785–1851)
Red Wing Starling, *ca. 1829*
From John James Audubon's
The Birds of America, *double-
elephant folio edition, 1827–1838*
*Hand-colored engraving with
etching and aquatint*
*The State Historical Society
of Missouri*

MEASUREMENTS
About 69.85 x 100.33 centimeters

REFERENCES
Desmond, Ray. *Great Natural
History Books and their
Creators*. London: The British
Library, 2003.

Duff, Hart Davis. *Audubon's
Elephant: America's Greatest
Naturalists and the Making of
"Birds of America."* New York:
H. Holt, 2004.

Fries, Waldemar H. *The Double
Elephant Folio: The Story of
Audubon's "Birds of America."*
Chicago: American Library
Association, 1973.

Souder, William. *Under a Wild
Sky: John James Audubon and
the Making of "The Birds of
America."* New York: North
Point Press, 2004.

In 1785, John James Audubon was born Jean Rabine in Saint-Domingue (now Haiti). He was the illegitimate son of a wealthy French sea captain. When he was formally adopted by his father, he was christened Jean Jacques Fougère Audubon (his name was later anglicized). He spent his childhood in France but fled to America in 1803 to avoid conscription into Napoleon's army. He became a citizen of the United States in 1812, and worked as a farmer, shopkeeper and mill owner in Pennsylvania, Kentucky, Missouri and Louisiana. In 1819, he declared bankruptcy and decided to make a living as an artist.

From an early age, Audubon had been interested in drawing and painting birds. Though self-taught, he learned to portray these winged creatures in minute ornithological detail. In order to convincingly represent living birds, he studied the creatures in their native habitats. Audubon carefully observed dead specimens and posed their bodies in lifelike positions on wire frameworks.

In 1826 Audubon traveled to Great Britain to find a printmaker who would help him create a book of large prints based on his ornithological studies. This four-volume tome, *The Birds of America*, was sold on subscription and included 435 plates. In order to make life-size images of all the birds, the engravings and etchings had to be printed on double-elephant folio sheets measuring approximately 39.5 by 28.5 inches. Edinburgh publisher William Lizars was initially hired to cut the plates, but he finished only ten before a colorist strike convinced Audubon to transfer his business to London publisher Robert Havell. Havell and his son, Robert Jr., engraved and etched the plates in copper and added tone with aquatint. Professional colorists then hand tinted each impression in watercolors. Since *The Birds of America* was produced at a time when copperplate intaglio printing was being gradually replaced by the cheaper techniques of lithography, steel engraving and wood engraving, it is one of the last major natural history books to be printed using the traditional engraving and etching process.

Between 1827 and 1838, Audubon periodically distributed *The Birds of America* prints to subscribers in eighty-seven "numbers" consisting of five prints each. Most subscribers paid for their own bindings although Audubon and Havell sold some bound copies. Between 1831 and 1839, Audubon also issued the five-volume *Ornithological Biography*, a book of text to accompany the prints. The book, published by Adam Black in Edinburgh, includes almost 500 entries that describe the appearances and habits of the birds pictured in the double-elephant folio edition. Audubon based his accounts on his close observation of the birds and lent authority to the text by hiring the Scottish naturalist William MacGillivray as his scientific editor.

In *Red Wing Starling* (pictured on the facing page), Audubon illustrates two adult and two immature red wing blackbirds. At the left, an adult female clings to the limb of a swamp maple while two immature birds perch on twigs below. The distinctive adult male swoops in from the right. Audubon had a characteristic interest in showing birds in motion (earlier ornithological artists tended to depict the creatures in static profiles). The lively arrangement of the birds creates the illusion that they are interacting with one another, which imposes a narrative element into the ornithological illustration.

JS

25

ICTERUS PHOENICEUS

REFERENCES
Desmond, Ray. *Great Natural
History Books and their
Creators*. London: The British
Library, 2003.

Duff, Hart Davis. *Audubon's
Elephant: America's Greatest
Naturalists and the Making of
"Birds of America."* New York:
H. Holt, 2004.

Fries, Waldemar H. *The Double
Elephant Folio: The Story of
Audubon's "Birds of America."*
Chicago: American Library
Association, 1973.

Rhodes, Richard. *John James
Audubon: The Making of an
American*. New York: Vintage
Books, 2006.

A rare, 1829 copy of John James Audubon's prospectus for *The Birds of America* is housed in Special Collections at Ellis Library. This pamphlet advertises the publication and describes its nature, scope, price and method of distribution. It explains that subscribers would receive the book as a series of "numbers" consisting of five plates each. The cost of each number was two guineas, or about twelve dollars. Each set would include one life-size engraving of one large bird.

Audubon's plates were grouped aesthetically rather than scientifically, so readers and viewers would have the sense that they were participating in an unpredictable "journey" through America to discover the country's birds. The book was not a scientific ornithology that was organized around the classifications of Linnaean taxonomy. As a Romantic artist, Audubon believed that his more random organization was not only more aesthetically pleasing but also a more realistic reflection of the unsystematic ways in which birds scattered themselves across the landscape in search of food and shelter.

During the twelve-year period that the double-elephant folio edition of *The Birds of America* was being produced, Audubon toured Great Britain, Europe and America to promote the book and seek new subscribers. He displayed early proofs of hand-colored prints, held exhibits of his original paintings, gave lectures and distributed copies of his prospectuses advertising the publication. The first prospectus was published in 1827 before the first fascicle, or "number," was issued. In it, the author distinguished his book from those of his contemporaries:

> *The author has not contented himself, as others have done, with single
> profile views, but in very many instances has grouped his figures so as
> to represent the originals in their natural avocations, and has placed
> them on branches of trees, decorated with foliage, blossoms and fruits or
> amidst plants of numerous species. Some are seen pursuing their prey
> through the air, searching for food amongst the leaves and herbage, sitting
> in their nests, or feeding their young; whilst others, of a different nature,
> swim, wade or glide in or over their allotted element* (Audubon, cited in
> Rhodes, 286).

The Ellis Library prospectus was circulated in 1829 after several of Audubon's bird prints had already been produced and distributed. It includes glowing reviews of the artist's work written by eminent individuals as well as a list of the book's subscribers as of 1829. This register of names, which includes the English king and other European royalty, provided potential customers with a list of people who endorsed the publication.

JS

Blue Heron

CATALOGUE 10
*John James Audubon
(American, 1785–1851)*
**The Birds of America: from
Drawings Made in the United
States and Their Territories**,
*1840–1844,
(Plate no. 372,* **Blue Heron**,
*pictured)
Printed text with hand-colored
lithographs
The State Historical Society
of Missouri*

MEASUREMENTS
26.35 x 16.51 centimeters (cover)

Despite John James Audubon's extensive marketing campaign, the cost of his double-elephant folio edition of *The Birds of America* limited its audience. At just over $1,000 per copy, only wealthy individuals and institutions could afford the giant luxury book. Fewer than 200 complete sets were produced, and the project failed to secure the ornithological artist's financial future.

Success eventually came when Audubon produced a royal octavo edition of *The Birds of America* in a smaller format at a more affordable price. With the aid of a *camera lucida* (a device that uses a glass prism to project a reduced image of an object onto a sheet of paper), Audubon, his sons and other hired artists made reduced line drawings of the large bird pictures. These sketches were then transferred onto litho stones and finished by lithographers in the firm of British-born printmaker John T. Bowen. R. Trembley and W.E. Hitchcock made most of the drawings on the stones. The plates were then printed, interspersed with text from the *Ornithological Biography* (see Cat. 8) and issued to subscribers in 100 fascicles or "numbers." Five plates were included in each number to make a total of 500 plates. Since there were only 435 plates in the double-elephant folio edition, new plates had to be made, and some of these were designed by Audubon's son, John Woodhouse Audubon. The octavo edition cost subscribers one dollar for each number or $100 for the entire book. When paid in installments, this price was affordable for many members of the American middle class. Over 1,000 people subscribed to the edition, and the book was such a resounding critical and financial success that Audubon called it his "Salvator."

Pictured above is the *Blue Heron* which is known today as the "little blue heron." It is plate 372 from the seventy-fifth "number" or fascicle of the octavo edition. It is thought that Audubon made the original watercolor for this print in 1832, and the artist's associate, George Lehman, painted the verdant landscape in the background. Lehman placed the bird in the wetlands of the American South. A tall clump of grass at the right mimics the beautiful tufted feathers of the heron's crown and neck. The blue-plumed bird dominates the composition as it advances forward and its head and neck are silhouetted against the sky. In the background stands an immature blue heron with white plumage. This bird was not in the original watercolor and was added by Havell (probably at Audubon's instruction) to the double-elephant folio engraving of the large heron. The lithographic artist later copied the white bird into the octavo edition plate.

JS

REFERENCES
Slatkin, Carole Anne. "Little Blue Heron," in *John James Audubon: The Watercolors for "The Birds of America."* Edited by Annette Blaugrund and Theodore E. Stebbins, Jr. New York: Villard books, Random House, 1993, 195–197.

Steiner, Bill. *Audubon Art Prints: A Collector's Guide to Every Early Edition.* Columbia, S.C.: University of South Carolina Press, 2003.

Tyler, Ron. *Audubon's Great National Work: The Royal Octavo Edition of "The Birds of America."* Austin: University of Texas Press, 1993.

CATALOGUE 11
*John T. Bowen and assistants
(British, 1801–ca. 1856)
After John James Audubon
(American, 1785–1851)*
**Bos Americanus, American
Bison or Buffalo**, *ca. 1845
From John James Audubon's*
**The Viviparous Quadrupeds of
North America**, *imperial folio
edition, 1842–1854
Hand-colored lithograph
The State Historical Society
of Missouri*

MEASUREMENTS
*About 53.34 x 68.58 centimeters
(sheet)*

REFERENCES
Audubon, John James.
*Audubon's Mammals: The
Quadrupeds of America
Complete and Unabridged.*
Secaucus, N.J.: Wellfleet Press,
2005.

Boehme, Sarah, ed. *John James
Audubon in the West. The Last
Expedition, Mammals of North
America.* New York: Harry
N. Abrams Inc, 2000. An
exhibition catalogue.

Steiner, Bill. *Audubon Art
Prints: A Collector's Guide to
Every Early Edition.* Columbia
S.C.: University of South
Carolina Press, 2003.

Tyler, Ron. "The Publication
of *The Viviparous Quadrupeds of
North America,*" in *John James
Audubon in the West. The Last
Expeditions, Mammals of North
America.* Edited by Sarah
Boehme. New York: Harry N.
Abrams Inc, 2000, 119–182.
An exhibition catalogue.

Not long after finishing *The Birds of America*, John James Audubon began *The Viviparous Quadrupeds of North America*. Published between 1842 and 1854, this book contained 150 hand-colored lithographs that represent viviparous American animals (animals that give birth to live young). The volumes were issued by subscription in thirty parts or "numbers." Each number contained five plates interleaved with text written by Audubon and his friend, the respected naturalist John Bachman. The imperial folio pages were smaller than the double-elephant folio sheets of *The Birds of America*. Even so, Audubon's *Quadrupeds* was one of the largest books ever printed in the United States; its unbound sheets measured twenty-eight by twenty-two inches.

Audubon's sons collaborated with him on the production of the book. John Woodhouse Audubon made about half of the animal studies, and Victor Gifford Audubon provided the backgrounds for most of the pictures. The Philadelphia firm of John T. Bowen, which was publishing the octavo edition of *The Birds of America*, made lithographs from the original animal paintings. Lithography was a relatively new printmaking technique that was less expensive and labor intensive than copperplate engraving. Bowen and his assistants carefully traced and copied the Audubon watercolors onto litho stones, and after the stones were printed, the impressions were hand tinted by professional colorists so that they closely resembled the original paintings. About 300 impressions of each print were produced by the Audubons.

The *American Bison* is plate 57 from the Imperial folio edition of *The Viviparous Quadrupeds of North America*. It is one of the earliest published images to accurately record the buffalo's appearance. Audubon positioned the animal so as to best display its characteristic anatomy and proportions. He carefully depicted the variations in the thickness of the buffalo's fur by articulating individual hairs and creating an expressive mass of wild, wind-swept locks around the animal's head.

The image fed into nineteenth-century Romantic notions about the American frontier. A single male buffalo stands in profile against a background of mountains, prairie and sky. Other members of the herd graze in the distance. Audubon created an iconic and almost heroic image of a quintessentially American animal. In the text of *The Viviparous Quadrupeds*, Bachman emphasized the perceived significance of the bison in the psyche of the nation. He said, "Whether we consider this noble animal as an object of the chase, or as an article of food for man, it is decidedly the most important of all our contemporary American quadrupeds . . ." In Audubon's print, the buffalo against the mountain backdrop is a symbol of the power and magnificence of the vast untamed American wilderness.

JS

Black American Wolf

CATALOGUE 12
*John James Audubon
(American, 1785–1851) and
John Bachman
(American, 1790–1874)*
**The Quadrupeds of North
America** *by John James Audubon
and the Rev. John Bachman,
1854–1855
(Plate no. 67,* **Black American
Wolf,** *pictured)
Printed text and hand-colored
lithographs with backgrounds
printed in color
Special Collections, Ellis Library
University of Missouri-Columbia*

MEASUREMENTS
27.5 x 19.5 centimeters (cover)

As the last of the large Imperial folio plates for John James Audubon's *The Viviparous Quadrupeds of North America* were being printed, John Woodhouse and Victor Gifford Audubon organized the production of a smaller royal octavo edition of the book with the shortened title *The Quadrupeds of North America*. The original illustrations for the *Viviparous Quadrupeds* were reduced using a *camera lucida* and copied onto litho stones. The order of the prints was rearranged slightly, and new lithographs were added. The 155 plates of the octavo edition were originally issued in thirty-one parts by subscription between 1849 and 1854. Each part or fascicle cost one dollar to make a total cost of thirty-one dollars.

The lithographs were printed by the publishing firms of John T. Bowen and Nagel and Weingaertner. Like the Imperial folio prints, they were hand colored although color backgrounds were also printed onto many sheets. About 2,000 copies of the first edition were produced, and later editions of undetermined size were issued in subsequent years by the Audubons. The plate pictured above comes from a copy of the book housed in Special Collections at Ellis Library. That copy dates from around 1854 or 1855. Another early edition is in the collection of The State Historical Society of Missouri.

The *Black American Wolf* was originally painted by John Woodhouse Audubon and copied onto the litho stone by W.E. Hitchcock. The plate was then hand painted so that its colors matched those of the original painting. An orange glow on the horizon suggests dusk or dawn, and a golden-eyed wolf leaps across the page. In the background (probably originally painted by Victor Gifford Audubon), a wolf pack chases three buffalo. With its nose lifted, tongue out and teeth bared, the foreground wolf may be joining in the hunt. None of the animal's four feet touch the ground. The image promotes the Romantic notion of the wild exoticism of the American West because its landscape is devoid of humans. The wolf is the embodiment of untamed Nature and the protagonist of an exhilarating drama of life, death and survival.

JS

REFERENCES
Audubon, John James.
*Audubon's Mammals: The
Quadrupeds of America
Complete and Unabridged.*
Secaucus, N.J.: Wellfleet Press,
2005.

Steiner, Bill. *Audubon Art
Prints: A Collector's Guide to
Every Early Edition.* Columbia,
S.C.: University of South
Carolina Press, 2003.

Tyler, Ron. "The Publication
of *The Viviparous Quadrupeds of
North America,*" in *John James
Audubon in the West. The Last
Expeditions, Mammals of North
America.* Edited by Sarah
Boehme. New York: Harry N.
Abrams Inc, 2000, 119–182.
An exhibition catalogue.

CATALOGUE 13
John T. Bowen and assistants
(British, 1801–ca. 1856)
After John James Audubon
(American, 1785–1851)
Common American Skunk,
ca. 1845
From John James Audubon's
The Viviparous Quadrupeds
of North America, *imperial*
folio edition, 1842–1854
Hand-colored lithograph
The State Historical Society
of Missouri

MEASUREMENTS
About 53.34 x 68.58 centimeters
(sheet)

REFERENCES
Audubon, John James.
Audubon and His Journals, with
Zoological and Other Notes by
Elliott Coues. Edited by Maria
Audubon. 2 vols. New York:
Charles Scribner's Sons, 1897.
Reprint, New York: Dover
Publications, 1994.

Boehme, Sarah. "Omega:
John James Audubon's Final
Artistic Journey," in *John*
James Audubon in the West.
The Last Expedition, Mammals
of North America. Edited
by Sarah Boehme. New
York: Harry N. Abrams Inc,
2000, 35–70. An exhibition
cataloague.

Rhodes, Richard. *John James*
Audubon: The Making of an
American. New York: Vintage
Books, 2006.

n 1827 entry in the journal of John James Audubon described the techniques he employed when he made his animal paintings:

No one, I think, paints in my method; . . . For instance, I am now working on a Fox; I take one neatly killed, put him up with wires and when satisfied with the truth of the position, I take my palette and work as rapidly as possible; the same with my birds. If practicable I finish the bird at one sitting–often, it is true, of fourteen hours, – so that I think they are correct, both in detail and composition." (John James Audubon, *Audubon and His Journals*, 202–20.)

Elsewhere in his writings, Audubon recorded the making of an animal study of two baby skunks. On June 9, 1842, he drew one male and one female skunk on his land in a rural part of what is now New York City. On January 22, 1843, he drew an adult female on the same property. The drawing of the young skunks was then glued below that of the adult animal, and the artist wrote instructions on the sheet for how the final image should be organized. Audubon stated that the older skunk was "to be placed on the rock, and the young beneath it, so as to render them almost unperceptible (sic) in the shadows" (Audubon, cited in Boehme, 47). The background artist (probably Victor Gifford Audubon) decided to perch the adult animal on a fallen tree rather than a rock with the hollowed wood sheltering the babies. The original drawing without the background is now preserved in the Pierpont Morgan Library in New York.

Audubon's *Common American Skunk* represents a family group with the mother assuming a protective stance against a perceived threat. She bares her teeth, squints her eyes and lifts her tail to expose her scent glands. The representation of this vicious aspect of the skunk alludes to the animal's propensity to squirt attackers with its noxious spray. Like many other animal images created in the Romantic era, Audubon's representation is somewhat anthropomorphized so as to encourage human empathy. The artist transforms the small mammal into a monumental and heroic creature and testifies to the ferocity of the maternal instinct. The postures of the young skunks display their more gentle dispositions as well as their juvenile markings and proportions.

JS

PLATE XLII.

Drawn from Nature by J. J. Audubon. F.R.S. F.L.S.

Lith. Printed & Col.d by J. T. Bowen, Phila.d 1844.

MEPHITIS AMERICANA, DESM.

CATALOGUE 14
Thomas McKenney
(American, 1785–1859) and
James Hall
(American, 1793–1868)
The History of the Indian Tribes
of North America, 1836–1844
(Plate no. 19, **Ki-on-twog-ky**,
pictured)
Printed text with hand-colored
lithographs
Special Collections, Ellis Library
University of Missouri-Columbia

MEASUREMENTS
52.5 x 38 centimeters (cover)

REFERENCES
Bowers, Shirley H. "Captured
on Canvas: McKenney-Hall's
*History of the Indian Tribes
of North America.*" *Florida
Historical Quarterly* 71 (1993),
339–347.

Horan, James David. *The
McKenney-Hall Portrait Gallery
of American Indians.* New York:
Bramhall House, 1986.

Cosentino, Andrew. *The
Paintings of Charles Bird King
(1785–1862).* Washington,
D.C.: Smithsonian Institution
Press for the National
Collection of Fine Arts, 1977.

Viola, Herman. *Thomas
L. McKenney: Architect of
America's Early Indian Policy,
1816-1830.* Chicago: Sage
Books, 1974.

Between 1816 and 1830, Thomas McKenney served as the United States Superintendent of Indian Trade (1816–1824) and the Commissioner of Indian Affairs (1824–1830). During his government tenure, he commissioned numerous portraits of Native Americans to be displayed in the Indian Gallery of the Department of War. After leaving office, he organized the publication of these portraits with biographical sketches and historical essays in *The History of the Indian Tribes of North America*. This book not only documents the vanishing culture of Native Americans from a European-American perspective, but it also serves as an early example of the high quality of nineteenth-century American book production and lithography.

The text of this three-volume tome was written by McKenney's associate, journalist James Hall, who had traveled extensively in the West. Most of the 120 illustrations were copied from paintings by Charles Bird King, the celebrated portraitist who painted many of the images in the War Department's Indian Gallery (selected portraits by Carl Bodmer, James Otto Lewis, P. Rhindesbacher and Robert Matthew Sully were also copied in McKenney's book). Although King never traveled west, he painted portraits of over one hundred Native Americans who visited the United States Capital between 1822 and 1842. Sadly, all but four of these paintings were destroyed in a fire at the Smithsonian Institution in 1865. McKenney's publication is the only surviving record of these historically important portraits.

The first folio edition of *The History of the Indian Tribes of North America* was published by subscription between 1836 and 1844. Edward C. Biddle issued the first installment, and subsequent sections were published by Frederick W. Greenough and the firm of Daniel Rice and James G. Clark. When the book first appeared, it was the most elaborate plate book ever produced in the United States. Several different artists and publishing houses were hired to make the plates by the relatively new process of lithography. The firms of Charles Hullmandel, Childs and Inman and John T. Bowen all printed lithographs for the book, which were then hand tinted by professional colorists.

McKenney's book was popular and was republished in several later folio editions. A cheaper, smaller octavo edition was issued in 1848 in which the plates were reduced by *camera lucida* and recopied by the firm of John T. Bowen. Bowen subsequently produced three more octavo editions of the book.

The image pictured here shows Kiontwogky, also known as Corn Plant or Cornplanter, a Seneca chief born ca. 1736. Kiontwogky's mother was Seneca and his father was white. He fought with the British during the American War of Independence and was a well-known orator and diplomat for the Seneca people. He died in Pennsylvania in 1836. The chief's plumed headdress, trade-silver jewelry and ceremonial pipe-tomahawk all indicate his high social status. This lithograph copied a lost painting by Charles Bird King, which was itself a copy. The original oil portrait, painted in 1796 by F. Bartoli, is now housed in the New York Historical Society.

JS

KI-ON-TWOG-KY

OR CORNPLANT

Philadelphia Published by E. C. Biddle.

Entered according to act of Congress in the year 1836 by E. C. Biddle in the Clerks office of the district Court of the Eastern district of Pa.

CATALOGUE 15
George Lehman
(American, ca. 1800–1870),
Peter S. Duval
(American, ca. 1800–1879)
and/or assistants
After Henry Inman
(American, 1801–1846) and
Charles Bird King
(American, 1785–1862)
Mohongo — Osage Woman,
ca. 1834
Early impression of an illustration
for Thomas McKenney and
James Hall's **The History of the
Indian Tribes of North America**
1836–1844
Hand-colored lithograph
The State Historical Society
of Missouri

MEASUREMENTS
20 x 14 centimeters (sheet)

In preparation for the publication of his book, *The History of the Indian Tribes of North America*, Thomas McKenney hired the young Philadelphia painter Henry Inman to copy Native American portraits from the United States War Department's Indian Gallery. These images were then recopied onto litho stones by artists working at several different printing firms. After the stones were printed, the impressions were hand colored in imitation of the original paintings. *Mohongo — Osage Woman*, drawn onto the litho stone by artists working in the firm of George Lehman and Peter Duval, was one of the earliest of the McKenney and Hall illustrations to be printed. This impression, made in 1834, preceded the first installation of *The History of the Indian Tribes of North America* by two years. Its circulation may have helped promote the publication, and later impressions were included in subsequent editions of the book.

Mohongo — Osage Woman presents a striking image of a Native American whose life was profoundly affected by her encounters with the Western world. Mohongo, also known as Myhangah or Mihonga, was a member of the Osage (Wazhazhe) Nation that originally lived along the Missouri and Osage Rivers in what is now the state of Missouri. In 1827, she was ill-used by the deceitful French entrepreneur David Delaunay who tricked her, her husband Kihegashugah and other members of the Osage into leaving their homes in the Chouteau camp on the Neosho River. Posing as a representative of the United States Government, Delaunay shipped the Native Americans to Europe where he exhibited them in a traveling wild west show. Mohongo and her husband were eventually abandoned in Paris, where Gilbert Motier, Marquis de Lafayette, took pity on them and paid for their passage home. Although her husband died of small pox during the return trip, Mohongo arrived safely in the United States in 1830. She was given the peace medal by President Andrew Jackson, and Thomas McKenney arranged to have Charles Bird King paint her portrait with her young child.

In the portrait, Mohongo wears a red-orange Western-style dress. Her pose is reminiscent of traditional Christian images of the Madonna and Child as she holds her baby close to her body. Both the mother and infant look out at the viewer, and the child clutches the Peace Medal that Mohongo wears around her neck. The iconography of the image promotes the idea that peaceful and positive relations between the United States Government and the Osage would continue in future generations. Unfortunately, the imagery does not reflect reality. In the second decade of the nineteenth century, as white settlers began to compete for their lands, the Osage people were forced to relocate to western Kansas, and in 1870 they were moved to their present home in Oklahoma.

JS

REFERENCES
Barratt, Carrie Rebora. *The Art of Henry Inman*. Washington, D. C.: Smithsonian Institution, 1987. An exhibition catalogue.

Biographical Dictionary of Indians of the Americas. 2 vols. Newport Beach, CA: American Indian Publishers Inc, 1991.

Mathews, John Joseph. *The Osages: Children of the Middle Waters*. Norman: University of Oklahoma Press, 1982.

Viola, Herman. *The Indian Legacy of Charles Bird King*. Washington, D. C.: Smithsonian Institution, 1976.

MO-HON-GO — OSAGE WOMAN.

CATALOGUE 16
Humphry Repton
(British, 1752–1818)
**Fragments on the Theory
and Practice of Landscape
Gardening**, *1816*
*(Foldout illustration between
pages 212 and 213, **central view
from the South and East Fronts
of the Cottage at Endsleigh,
Devonshire–Duchess of
Bedford**, pictured)*
*Special Collections, Ellis Library
University of Missouri-Columbia*

MEASUREMENTS
35.5 x 29 centimeters (cover)

Humphry Repton was England's first self-proclaimed professional "landscape gardener," a term he coined himself. During the eighteenth century, English gardeners began to break away from the formalized symmetry and geometrical patterns of past garden designs. Instead, the new garden style focused on creating bucolic and picturesque views that emulated landscape paintings. Emphasis was placed on the creation of broad, sweeping lawns, attractive groupings of trees, curving paths and water features such as ponds and streams. Ornamental plantings were rigidly controlled and made to look as if they were natural features. Creating "natural" scenery too perfect to exist in nature, Repton and other gardeners of this period sought to shape the landscape without the outward appearance of control.

Repton's main employment was as a design consultant for wealthy landowners throughout the English countryside, and he used his artistic and writing skills in unprecedented ways to further his career. When Repton designed a garden, he visited the property in order to sketch, survey and get an idea of what the landowner wanted. After formulating his design, he usually presented his client with a manuscript of his plans bound in red morocco. These "red books" included full written descriptions of the landscape and maps, plans and watercolor illustrations. Repton devised a way to make the illustrations interact with the client by incorporating overlays that, when closed, showed the current state of the property. The client could lift the overlay to see how his or her estate would look after the proposed modification. Written in polite prose, Repton's suggestions and innovative illustrations charmed his clients and ensured that he remained in high demand even if his plans were not always carried out.

Repton aimed to follow in the footsteps of the most prominent gardener of the previous generation, Lancelot "Capability" Brown, who had transformed large estates throughout England. In some cases Repton was called in to enhance Brown's landscapes by adding or adjusting individual features. He reintroduced formal elements such as terraces, trellises and flower gardens and also became known for themed and novelty gardens. While Brown made his name by doing large-scale overhauls of entire estates, Repton became famous for his fine-tuning and attention to detail.

Although Repton took on hundreds of commissions during his thirty-year career, his writings and watercolors are his most enduring achievements. His illustrations, written commentary and explanations of his design principles, were collected and published as *Observations on the Theory and Practice of Landscape Gardening* (1803) and *Fragments on the Theory and Practice of Landscape Gardening* (1816). As in the red books, the color plates in Repton's publications incorporate flaps and overlays. The images pictured on the facing page show views of the grounds at the Dutchess of Bedford's cottage at Endsleigh–Devonshire. With the overlays closed, one sees the grounds before Repton's improvements. With the overlays open, one sees Repton's proposed landscaping work.

Not only did the books solidify Repton's reputation as England's foremost landscape gardener, they also provided unprecedented records of eighteenth-century English landscape design for subsequent generations. No previous landscape gardener had ever written so much about his craft.

KBH

REFERENCES
Batey, Mavis. "The Picturesque: An Overview." *The Picturesque* 22, no. 2 (winter 1994): 121–32.

Hyams, Edward. *Capability Brown and Humphry Repton.* London: Dent, 1971.

Repton, Humphry. *The Red Books of Humphry Repton.* London: Basilisk Press, 1976.

Stroud, Dorothy. *Humphry Repton.* London: Country Life, 1962.

GENERAL VIEW FROM THE SOUTH AND EAST FRONTS OF THE COTTAGE AT ENDSLEIGH, DEVONSHIRE. — DUTCHESS OF BEDFORD

With overlay closed

GENERAL VIEW FROM THE SOUTH AND EAST FRONTS OF THE COTTAGE AT ENDSLEIGH, DEVONSHIRE. — DUTCHESS OF BEDFORD

With overlay open

CATALOGUE 17
Daniel Havell
(British, d. 1826?)
After Henry Salt
(British, 1780–1827)
A View at Lucknow,
From **Twenty-Four views taken in St. Helena, the Cape, India, Ceylon, Abyssinia, and Egypt**,
1809
Hand-colored etching and aquatint
Museum of Art and Archaeology University of Missouri-Columbia
Gift of Mr. Stuart Borchard
63.32.8

MEASUREMENTS
54.5 x 74.5 centimeters (sheet)

REFERENCES
Archer, Mildred. *Early Views of India: The Picturesque Journeys of Thomas and William Daniell, 1786–1794; The Complete Aquatints.* New York: Thames and Hudson, 1980.

Caine, William Sproston. *Picturesque India: A Handbook for European Travelers; Illustrations Drawn by John Pedder, H. Sheppard Dale, and H.H. Stanton.* London: G. Routledge, 1890. Reprint, 1982.

Leask, Negel. *Curiosity and the Aesthetics of Travel Writing, 1770–1840: 'From an Antique Land.'* Oxford: Oxford University Press, 2002.

Mountnorris, George Annesley. *Voyages and Travels in India, Ceylon, the Red Sea, Abyssinia and Egypt in the Years 1802, 1803, 1804, 1805, and 1806.* 3 vols. London: William Miller, 1809.

European exploration and colonization of the Americas, Africa and India engendered interest in picturesque travel books in the nineteenth century. These illustrated texts reflected interest in Romanticized representations of exotic lands, and they often contained color pictures and extensive accounts of the culture, dress, habits and architecture of the people living in countries outside Europe. This print comes from *Twenty-Four views taken in St. Helena, the Cape, India, Ceylon, Abyssinia, and Egypt,* an excellent early example of a sumptuously illustrated English travel book. The massive tome originally included twenty-four large plates that represented Asian and African cities. It rivaled the magnificence of one of the earliest picturesque travel books, *Oriental Scenery* (1795–1808), by Thomas and William Daniell.

The printmaker Daniel Havell based this hand-colored aquatint, *A View at Lucknow*, on a watercolor by the artist Henry Salt. Salt was born in Lichfield, Staffordshire, England, in 1780. He trained as a portrait painter at the British Royal Academy and studied drawing and painting under Joseph Farington (1747–1821) and John Hoppner (1758–1810). However, Salt's career path changed when he was appointed as secretary and draughtsman to George Annesley, Viscount Valentia (and later Lord Mountnorris), with whom he traveled to Africa in 1802 and India in 1803. In 1805 Salt and Valentia embarked on an extensive tour of the Abyssinian highlands. During their travels, Salt made numerous landscape watercolor drawings to record the monuments he encountered, and after his return to England in 1806, many of these drawings were made into prints that were used to illustrate Valentia's *Voyages and Travels to India*, published in 1809. To accompany Valentia's text, William Miller published a second more monumental volume of illustrations, *Twenty-four views taken in St. Helena, the Cape, India, Ceylon, Abyssinia, and Egypt.* Robert Havell directed the production of the aquatint plates, which were engraved and etched by the printmakers Daniel Havell, John Bluck and J. Hill. Professional colorists in Havell's employment then hand tinted the prints. The illustrations in this book are now considered to be some of the best early nineteenth-century visual records of east Asian countries by Europeans, and they are also some of the earliest printed representations of Abyssinia. Havell's firm continued to play an important role in the publication of illustrated books during the first half of the nineteenth century. During this period, for example, the firm supervised the engravings for John James Audubon's *The Birds of America* (Cat. 8).

View of Lucknow features an Indian city situated on the bank of the Gomti River. The urban center was founded by the nawabs of Oudh during the period of Mughal rule in India. The fourth of the ten nawabs, Asaf-ud-Daula, moved his court to Lucknow and renovated and rebuilt the city. Thomas and William Daniell visited Lucknow during this period, but by the time Salt arrived in the city, it was ruled by Saadat-Ali-Khan, a son of Asaf-ud-Daula, who ceded half of Awadh Kingdom to the British in 1801.

The print also depicts the Fort of Machhi Bhawan, built on the Lakshman Tia mound, and the Mosque of Aurangzeb. Viscount Valentia wrote that the mosque was "built of brick but is completely covered with so brilliant a chunam, that it is impossible to bear the luster when the sun shines full upon it." The distinctly Indian architecture towering in the background, the elephant in the foreground, the costumes and the vegetation are all exotic elements that help construct a Romantic impression of India for European audiences.

SC

A VIEW AT LUCKNOW.

The Literary World

Joan Stack
Associate Curator

*Museum of Art and Archaeology
University of Missouri-Columbia*

The material nature of literary books can profoundly affect the reader's experience of the texts. Whether viewers are looking at an original manuscript or a sumptuously illustrated printed volume, they will find that their interpretations of the written words will be influenced by the arrangement of visual elements on the page. Illustrations make ideas concrete and guide readers' imaginations. Fiction illustrators often adapt their style to reflect the expressive and emotional nature of the books they illustrate. Encouraging readers to equate the beauty and energy of the pictures with that of the words, good illustrators create images that enhance the literary qualities of their books.

Most of the books and artwork in this section of the catalogue date from the nineteenth and early twentieth centuries. They represent some of the most important aesthetic and intellectual movements of the period, from Neoclassicism to Romanticism to Social Realism. They also embody the new technical innovations of the industrial age as well as new ideas about the nature and function of books as aesthetic objects.

CATALOGUE 18
William Blake
(British, 1757–1827)
Job's Evil Dreams, *from*
Illustrations of the Book of Job*,*
1821–1826
Line engraving
Museum of Art and Archaeology
University of Missouri-Columbia
81.49

MEASUREMENTS
50.5 x 34.5 centimeters (sheet)

REFERENCES
Bindman, David. *Blake as an Artist.* Oxford: E. P. Dutton; Phaidon, 1977.

Damon, S. Foster. *Blake's Job: William Blake's Illustrations of the Book of Job.* Providence, R. I.: Brown University Press, 1966.

Eaves, Morris, ed. *The Cambridge Companion Guide to William Blake.* Cambridge: Cambridge University Press, 2003.

King, James. *William Blake: His Life.* New York: St. Martin's Press, 1991.

Raine, Kathleen. *The Human Face of God: William Blake and the Book of Job.* New York: Thames and Hudson, 1982.

Vaughan, William. *William Blake.* Princeton, New Jersey: Princeton University Press, 1999.

Although the visionary art of English poet and artist William Blake is widely admired today, it was not fully appreciated during the age of Enlightenment in which the artist lived. Profoundly interested in the Bible, Blake was a deeply religious man who used scripture as a primary source of inspiration in his poetry and artwork. From an early age, the artist reported seeing visions of otherworldly forms that intermingled with living people. These visions continued throughout his lifetime, and they strengthened his spiritual beliefs and inspired his artwork and poetry.

In 1825 John Linnell commissioned the engravings for the *Illustrations of the Book of Job*, which provided Blake, who was sixty-five years old at the time, with crucial financial support. The artist based the engravings on a set of watercolors he had made previously for Thomas Butts. Blake traced the watercolors, reproduced the images onto metal plates and printed them on India paper. From the first edition, 315 copies were offered for sale to the public.

In the story of Job, Satan strikes a deal with God over Job, who is portrayed as the ideal God-fearing man. God allows Satan to test Job by subjecting him to years of torment and suffering. *Job's Evil Dreams* represents the turning point during Job's trial when the tormented protagonist recognizes that his alleged God is actually the Devil. The figure who hovers above Job is the God of Justice. The snake of materialism is intertwined with this God, whose hoofed left foot exposes him as Satan in disguise. In the upper corner, the lightning of damnation surges from his right hand as he points to the stone tablets of the Law. His left hand points below to Hell where damned souls try to pull Job into the flames.

SC

CATALOGUE 19
John Flaxman
(British, 1755–1826)
Orestes Killing Clytemnestra
or **Behold the Proud Oppressors**
of My Country, *ca. 1793*
Gray ink over graphite
Museum of Art and Archaeology
University of Missouri-Columbia
62.8

MEASUREMENTS
23.5 x 29.8 centimeters (sheet)

CATALOGUE 20
John Flaxman
(British, 1755–1826)
Thomas Piroli
(Italian, 1752–1824) and
Frank Howard
(British, 1805–1866)
Compositions for the Tragedies
of Aeschylus
(Plate no. 26, **Behold the Proud**
Opressors of My Country*,*
pictured)
1831 (first published in 1795)
Engravings
Special Collections, Ellis Library
University of Missouri-Columbia

MEASUREMENTS
26.5 x 42.5 centimeters (cover)

CATALOGUE 19

The British artist John Flaxman was a pioneer of the neoclassical style in England. He traveled frequently to Rome and was inspired by ancient reliefs and drawings on Greek and Roman pottery. In the late eighteenth century, he was well-known for designing figural decorations for ceramics produced by Josiah Wedgewood. He was also a renowned book illustrator who was celebrated for his crisp, linear style. This style was well-suited to classical texts and to the European taste of the period. Flaxman seems to have conceived his illustrations as visual translations of verbal texts that replace rather than illustrate the words. When the compositions were first published, they were issued as collections of engravings. These picture books were made to tell their stories non-verbally.

The drawing (Cat. 19) and the engraving (Cat. 20) *Orestes Killing Clytemnestra* record one of thirty designs commissioned by the dowager Countess Spencer to illustrate a book of collected scenes from the tragedies of the Greek author Aeschylus. The first edition of *Compositions for the Tragedies of Aeschylus* was published in 1795 by Jane Matthews, Flaxman's aunt and a commercial print and bookseller. The drawings were engraved in Rome by Tammaso Piroli, a printmaker who worked in the shop of Giovanni Battista Piranesi. In 1831 *Compositions for the Tragedies of Aeschylus* was republished posthumously by Flaxman's wife and Maria Denman. English printmaker Frank Howard engraved four previously unpublished compositions for this edition, a copy of which is housed in Special Collections at Ellis Library.

The episode illustrated in both the drawing and print comes from Act Three of Aeschylus' play *Choephoroi* (*The Libation Bearers*). Orestes, the son of King Agamemnon, stands over the corpses of Clytemnestra, his mother, and her lover, Aegisthus, while the Chorus looks on at right. The adulterous pair had killed Agamemnon when he returned from Troy, and Orestes felt compelled to avenge his father's death. Below the engraved image is a translation of words spoken by Orestes as he gestured toward the bodies. He says, "Behold the proud oppressors of my country."

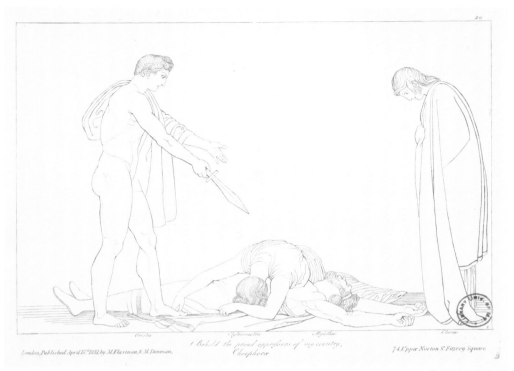

In the left corner of Flaxman's preliminary drawing, there is a tiny compositional study of the arrangement of the primary figures. Perhaps these were the first lines made on the sheet. After determining the elements of the general arrangement, Flaxman probably sketched his composition in pencil. He then retraced selected graphite lines in ink. Upon close examination, the viewer can see how the artist adjusted his design as he drew.

It is unclear whether this is the final study for Piroli's print or a drawing made in preparation for the final study. The engraving *Orestes Killing Clytemestra* in *Compositions for the Tragedies of Aeschylus* is very close to the Museum of Art and Archaeology's sketch, but there are important differences. The drapery and hair of the Chorus have been altered, and the draped hand has been raised. The hair of all the figures is more carefully articulated in the engraving, and so are the beard and clothing of Aegisthus. Moreover, Piroli made subtle changes in the character of Flaxman's design. In the drawing, Orestes' eyes seem to open wide with rage. Although the engraver copies this expression, his lines do not capture the emotion with the same intensity. Also, by slightly changing the articulation of the muscles of Orestes' shoulder and arms, Piroli created a more powerful figure, which de-emphasized the youthfulness of Agamemnon's son.

JS

REFERENCES

Eddy, Linda R. "Achilles Contending with the Rivers: Flaxman Translates Homer." *The Stanford Museum*, 6–7 (1976–1977): 10–17.

Johnson, Deborah. *Old Master Drawings from the Museum of Art, Rhode Island School of Design*. Providence, R. I.: Rhode Island School of Design, 1983.

Whinney, Margaret. "Flaxman and the Eighteenth Century," *Journal of the Warburg Courtauld Institute* 19 (1956): 269–282.

CATALOGUE 21

In 1805 London publishers John and Josiah Boydell issued two atlas folio volumes titled *A Collection of Prints from Pictures for the Purpose of Illustrating the Dramatic Works of Shakespeare by the Artists of Great Britain*. This monumental tome contained 100 original line and stipple engravings, often with preliminary etching. In 1852 the book was published in the United States after a wealthy American dentist, Shearjashub Spooner, acquired the engraved plates. Because over a thousand impressions had been made from them in Boydell's time, Spooner hired craftsmen to re-cut and re-etch the originals. The enterprising dentist republished the prints in New York under the title *The American Edition of Boydell's Illustrations of the Dramatic Works of Shakespeare* (Cat. 21). This edition faithfully reproduced the original publication although the order of the illustrations was changed.

Both the British and American editions of this book document a collection of paintings commissioned by John Boydell and displayed at the celebrated Shakespeare Gallery in Pall Mall, London, between 1789 and 1805. The plate illustrated in Cat. 21 represents the allegorical sculpture of Shakespeare by Thomas Banks (1735–1805) that decorated the facade of the building. Inside the Shakespeare Gallery, visitors encountered original artwork by some of Britain's most celebrated native and foreign artists including Sir Joshua Reynolds, George Romney, Benjamin West, Angelica Kaufman and Henry Fuseli. At the exhibition hall, one could purchase *A Catalogue of the Pictures in the Shakespeare Gallery, Pall Mall* (see Cat. 22). This little book advertised subscriptions for prints made after the paintings and listed the exhibited artworks.

Each entry also supplied appropriate excerpts from the Shakespeare plays that were illustrated in the gallery.

The proprietor of the establishment was John Boydell, a wealthy and successful publisher of prints who also served as Lord Mayor of London in 1790. Although Boydell charged admission to his gallery, he planned to make most of his profit by selling subscriptions for reproductions of his Shakespeare paintings. Subscribers would pay an initial fee and would periodically receive small sets of four prints, called "numbers." Payment for the entire collection was made in installments upon receipt of each number. When the complete set of prints had been received, and sometimes before, the prints could be bound into books. By the time the Shakespeare Gallery opened in 1789, Boydell had over 600 subscribers for the reproduced engravings. The first numbers were issued in the 1790s.

Boydell hired the finest graphic artists in England to copy his Shakespeare paintings. Although some printmakers worked in the time-consuming line-engraving technique, most employed the faster stipple process either by itself or in combination with line work. The stipple technique, which builds subtle layers of tone with patterns of dots, was particularly effective in replicating the painterly qualities of the original artwork.

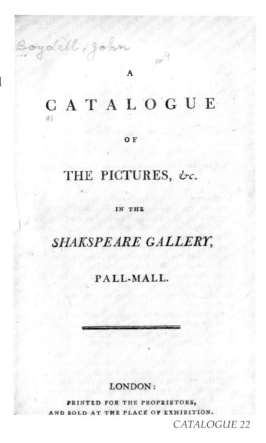

CATALOGUE 22

The making of the plates was a long and tedious process for which the artists were well compensated. The engravers were paid better than the painters because their craft was much more time consuming. In total, Boydell paid just over 17,045 pounds to his painters, but his engravers received 25,926 pounds.

Unfortunately, Boydell lost money on his investment. The once-prosperous reproductive print business collapsed at the beginning of the nineteenth century when wars in France and Spain closed off the continental market. Also, as the neo-classical style became more and more popular in Europe, the fashion for painterly stipple prints began to wane in favor of traditional line engravings. Deep in debt, Boydell acquired Parliamentary permission in 1804 to hold a lottery in which he offered the paintings of the Shakespeare Gallery as the grand prize. Unfortunately, the well-known publisher died in December of that year, but the lottery raised 45,000 pounds and allowed his nephew and heir, Josiah Boydell, to settle his uncle's debts. Flush with money, Josiah offered the winner of the lottery, Mr. Tassie, 10,000 pounds to buy back the Shakespeare paintings. Tassie demanded 25,000 pounds to return the prize, and since the younger Boydell was unable to pay such a large sum, Christie's was hired to auction the collection on May 17, 1805. The artwork sold for 6,181 pounds, much less than John Boydell had originally paid for them.

JS

REFERENCES

Friedman, Winifred. *Boydell's Shakespeare Gallery*. New York and London: Garland Publishing Inc, 1976.

Hamlyn, Robin. "The Shakespeare Galleries of John Boydell and James Woodmason," in *Shakespeare in Art*. Edited by Jane Martineau. London and New York: Merell Publishers, 2003, 97–101. An exhibition catalogue.

Pape, Walter, and Frederick Burwick, eds. *Boydell's Shakespeare Gallery*. Essen and Bottrop: Peter Pomp, 1996.

CATALOGUE 23
Jean Pierre Simon
(British, ca. 1750–ca. 1825)
After Henry Fuseli
(Swiss, 1741–1825)
The Enchanted Island before
the Cell of Prospero—Prospero,
Miranda, Caliban and Ariel,
Act I, Scene II of The Tempest,
1797
*From **A Collection of Prints***
from Pictures for the Purpose
of Illustrating the Dramatic
Works of Shakespeare by the
***Artists of Great Britain**, 1803*
(preface dated 1805)
Stipple and line engraving
Museum of Art and Archaeology
University of Missouri-Columbia
87.128

MEASUREMENTS
50.5 x 66 centimeters (sheet)

Johann Heinrich Füssli, known in England as Henry Fuseli, was born in Switzerland in 1741. A literate and well-read intellectual, he became an ordained minister in the Swiss Reformed Church. In 1763 he settled in London, but after Sir Joshua Reynolds encouraged the young minister to become a painter in 1768, the Swiss artist spent the following eight years of his life in Italy studying the art of ancient Rome and the heroic paintings of Michelangelo and Raphael. After a brief stay in Zürich, he settled in London during the spring of 1779.

Fuseli considered himself a history painter and favored artwork of grandiose size. He merged a neoclassical, heroic style with a passionate interest in unearthly visions and Romantic subject matter. Fuseli's fantastic imagination was often inspired by dreams, visions and dramatic literature. His celebrated 1781 painting, *The Nightmare,* became an iconic image almost immediately after it was painted.

The original painting *The Enchanted Island before the Cell of Prospero* was one of nine pictures that Fuseli made for Boydell's Shakespeare Gallery (see Cat. 21 and Cat. 22). The now lost artwork measured eight by eleven and a half feet and illustrated an episode from Act I, Scene II of Shakespeare's *The Tempest*. While Fuseli's fantastic imagination conjured up the characters of the play's mystical isle, the artist added classical gravitas to the composition with visual quotations from antiquity and the oeuvre of Michelangelo.

Jean-Pierre Simon's stipple engraving recorded the lost work. In the left foreground, the elderly magician Prospero confronts his monstrous servant Caliban and accuses the creature of attempting to molest Miranda, the aging sorcerer's daughter. The lovely Miranda is shielded by her father as she turns away from her grotesque admirer. Prospero, dressed in prophet-like robes, is shown in profile, and his visage is remote and commanding. He stretches out an authoritative, Michelangelesque arm towards Caliban, and the naked monster responds by extending his own closed-fisted and defiant arm. This compositional pastiche of Michelangelo's *Creation of Adam* emphasizes the distance rather than the nearness of the protagonists' hands. Instead of infusing Caliban with the spirit of humanity, the god-like Prospero curses the misshapen, inhuman creature. Caliban becomes an anti-Adam; the beauty of his upper body, a reflection of the *Torso Belvedere*, is subverted by his grotesque face and distended nipples. This half-human beast, with his dark complexion and gargoyle-like visage, is not only a cruel caricature of Michelangelo's Adam but also a cousin of the demons that torment the lost souls in the Sistine master's *Last Judgment*.

The Shakespearian episode illustrated in the picture is quoted at length in the catalogue for the gallery (Cat. 22). Viewers who read that text as they viewed the painting could imagine the dialogue between Prospero and Caliban. However, in the print the text below the image quotes only Prospero as he announces Caliban's punishment:

> *For this, be sure, to-night thou shall have cramps,*
> *Side-stitches that shall pen thy breath up; urchins*
> *Shall for that vast of night that they may work,*
> *All exercise on thee: thou shalt be pinch'd*
> *As thick as honey-combs, each pinch more stinging*
> *Than bees that made them.*

The lobster near Caliban's right foot foreshadows the malformed servant's nighttime fate. The sea creature reaches toward the unfortunate fiend and opens its large pincers.

After the closing of the Shakespeare Gallery, the painting sold at auction in 1805 to John Green. The artwork was subsequently destroyed, and only a fragment that displays the head and torso of Prospero survives in the York City Art Gallery in Britain. The print commissioned by Boydell is the only surviving record of Fuseli's composition.

Little is known about British printmaker Jean-Pierre Simon who made this graphic copy of *The Enchanted Island before the Cell of Prospero*. Scholars believe that

he was born in around 1750 and that he was the student of Francesco Bartolozzi, an Italian émigré who is thought to have invented the popular stipple engraving technique. Simon was a master of this time-consuming printmaking process, which combined elements of etching and engraving. He received many commissions and made fifteen prints after paintings in the Shakespeare Gallery.

Since stippling could effectively imitate painterly effects, the process was often used to create prints from paintings in the eighteenth and early nineteenth centuries. In Simon's time, a stipple artist began with a copper plate covered with an asphaltum ground. He or she then incised a complex series of tiny holes into the ground with a stipple graver, hammer punch or roulette. The plate was then placed in an acid bath, which bit through the small holes and produced a pitted surface. This surface was usually reworked and refined using traditional engraving techniques.

Simon's stippling captures some of the painterly mysticism of Fuseli's lost composition. Delicate dot patterns depict the frothy ocean, misty air and ephemeral body of Ariel hovering between Prospero and Caliban. The artist also used traditional line engraving to articulate the dark shadows and model forms in the foreground (see, for example, the representation of Prospero's drapery). These engraved lines create an impression of material solidity that contrasts with the illusion of transient light and the otherworldly atmosphere in the background.

JS

REFERENCES

Lennox-Boyd, Christopher. "The Prints Themselves: Production, Marketing, and their Survival," in *Boydell's Shakespeare Gallery*. Edited by Walter Pape and Frederick Burwick. Essen and Bottrop: Peter Pomp, 1996, 45–53.

Weinglass, David H. *Prints and Engraved Illustrations By and After Henry Fuseli*. Aldershot: Scolar Press, 1994.

De temps en temps j'aime a voir le vieux Pere,
Et je me garde bien de lui rompre en Visiere.

The novelist and playwright Johann Goethe published part one of *Faust, a Tragedy* in 1808. In Goethe's tale, the devil, Mephistopheles, appears as a gentleman courtier who agrees to serve the alchemist Faust on earth if Faust will serve him in the afterlife. With Mephistopheles at his side, Faust is magically transformed into a young man. He revels in his newfound youth and seduces and impregnates the beautiful Margaret, nicknamed Gretchen, and eventually kills her avenging brother with Satan's assistance. A fallen woman, Gretchen goes mad and is condemned to death after drowning her baby. When Faust realizes he is responsible for his lover's suffering, he attempts to convince her to escape from prison. Gretchen, however, is resigned to her fate and refuses to go with him. The play ends as a chorus of angels announce that Gretchen is saved.

In 1828 the lithographer and publisher Charles Etienne Pierre Motte collaborated with Eugène Delacroix to produce a new, deluxe edition of *Faust* that included a French translation of Goethe's text by Albert Stapfer and eighteen lithographs by the artist. The thirty-year-old Delacroix was known for his passionate imagery and his interest in representing scenes of violence and the supernatural. He had caused sensations in the Parisian art world with paintings such as *Dante and Virgil in Hell* (1822) and *The Massacre at Chios* (1824). His affinity for literary subjects and passion for drama made him an ideal candidate to illustrate *Faust*, and his visionary interpretations of the play won the approval of the aging Goethe. After seeing early proofs of the lithographs, the German author said to his friend Johann Eckermann, "M. Delacroix is a man of great talent who found in *Faust* his proper aliment. The French censure his wildness, but it suits him well here," (Goethe, *Conversations with Eckerman*, 108).

Mephistopheles in the Air (Cat. 24) illustrates an early scene in the play from the "Prologue in Heaven." In the prologue, God converses with Mephistopheles, and the two make a wager: the devil bets that he can win Faust's soul while God asserts that Faust will eventually be saved. Delacroix pictures Mephistopheles in his demonic avatar before the fiend takes on the guise of a handsome gentleman later in the play. Gesturing and grinning, perhaps in conversation with God, the devil flies over the hazy profile of a city. The creature's nude, dark-skinned body is beautifully proportioned, yet his Pan-like face and claws reveal his inhuman nature (the devil's distinctive profile is a consistent aspect of his appearance in the lithographs that follow). Below the airborne demon, the sun sets behind the spire of a church. This iconography appropriately initiates a literary journey that explores the dark side of the human psyche.

Delacroix illustrated *Faust* with a series of prints that were innovative both artistically and technically. The lithographs were drawn directly on the stone by the artist, who was a leader in the development of this relatively new printmaking technique. Rarely leaving any area of his stones untouched, he covered their surfaces with beautiful crayon drawings that made full use of the tonal range between black and white. Various shades of gray acted as middle tones that heightened the contrast between the velvety darks and the luminous highlights. This technique allowed the artist to produce the kind of dramatic *chiaroscuro* in his prints that he was able to create in his paintings. Delacroix also experimented with a variety of drawing techniques. Sometimes he shaded areas of the stone with the side of his litho crayon and other times built up complex matrices of hatched and cross-hatched lines. He rubbed his drawings to create hazy atmospheric effects and scratched back into his blacks and grays to create vivid highlights. The animated, gestural quality of his lines and his masterful control of light and shadow added energy and drama to his images.

The Duel of Faust and Valentine (Cat. 25, page 50) represents a dramatic moment in the middle of Goethe's play. Margaret's brother, Valentine, had vowed to avenge the loss of his sister's honor after he learned that Faust had seduced her. Faust and Valentine are fighting a duel, and Mephistopheles has interfered by parrying one of Valentine's blows and allowing Faust to inflict a fatal wound. Delacroix represented the moment when Faust strikes, and he captured the dramatic energy of the scene with a dynamic composition organized around a series of diagonals.

In *The Shade of Margaret Appearing to Faust* (Cat. 26, page 51), Delacroix created a quintessentially Romantic image in which he blurred the lines between reality and imagination. Like many nineteenth-century artists, he was interested in the problem of representing unearthly worlds and visions. Here he pictured a scene that takes place during a witches' Sabbath on Walpurgis Night. Mephistopheles has invited Faust to this diabolic festival in the Harz Mountains. Among the ghoulish revelers, Faust sees an apparition of his lover Margaret with her throat slit and her body supported by grinning demons. Snakes, lizards and grotesque creatures surround the hallucination while other beings lurk in the shadows. The artist's lively and expressive drawing style enhances the chaotic drama of the lithograph.

JS

REFERENCES
Jobert, Barthélémy, ed. *Delacroix: Le trait romantique.* Paris: Bibliothèque nationale de France, 1998. An exhibition catalogue.

Goethe, Johann Wolfgang von. *Conversations with Eckerman.* Translated by John Oxenford. London: 1850. Reprint, San Francisco: North Point Press, 1984.

Marqusee, Michael. "Introduction," in *Faust with Eighteen Lithographs by Eugène Delacroix.* New York: Paddington Press, 1977.

Sérullaz, Arlette. "Un parcours initiatique. Delacroix illustrateur de *Faust*," in *Faust.* Edited by Diane de Selliers. Paris: Diane de Selliers, 1997, 11–20.

Delacroix inv.t et Lithog

Meph — Bourre . . Val . of ? . . Meph — Voila mon rustaud apprivoisé

CATALOGUE 27
Jean Ignace Isidore Gérard
Known as J. J. Grandville
(French, 1803–1847) and
Taxile Delord
(French, 1815–1877)
Les Fleurs animées, *1847*
(Cover and illustration for page
no. 8, **Dahlia**, *pictured)*
Printed text with hand-colored
engravings and wood engraved
frontispieces
Special Collections, Ellis Library
University of Missouri-Columbia

MEASUREMENTS
26.2 x 18.5 centimeters (cover)

Jean Ignace Isidore Gérard adopted the surname of his grandparents, Grandville, when he began publishing his drawings in the 1820s. The artist was the son of a French miniature painter, and as a young man, he worked as a political caricaturist. Like his contemporary, Honoré Daumier, he contributed to various French periodicals, including *La Caricature* and *Le Charivari*. In 1835 the French government imposed laws that censored politically oriented caricatures, and Grandville turned his satirical eye to society. The artist had already established a reputation as a keen social satirist with *Les Métamorphoses du jour*, published in 1828 and 1829. *Les Métamorphoses* consisted of seventy pictures of creatures with the bodies of men and women and the heads of animals. Grandville endowed the faces of these creatures with distinctly human expressions as they acted out a comedy of manners.

In the 1840s Grandville displayed his bizarre and fertile imagination in several collaborations with the writer Taxile Delord. In 1844 the two Frenchmen produced *Un autre monde*, a book dominated by strange images that sometimes recall those of Hieronymus Bosch. *Les Fleurs animées*, known in English as *The Flowers Personified*, was a later collaboration with Delord. It was published in 1847, the year of Grandville's death. It too presented a weird, whimsical and dreamlike world. Flowers, transformed into tiny women, are draped in petals and leaves and interact with the animals and insects of the garden. The text tells a story of woodland magic in which a fairy magically anthropomorphizes the garden plants. The whimsical, absurd and sometimes surprising drawings reflect Romantic and sentimental attitudes toward nature and the landscape. Alphonse Karr wrote two introductory essays for the book, and L. F. Raban (under the pseudonym Comte Foelix) added a section titled "Ladies' Horticulture," which discusses the flowers on a more straightforward, scientific level.

Grandville and his assistants made over fifty drawings for *Les Fleurs animées*, and many of these survive in the Bibliothèque municipale in Nancy, France. Most of Grandville's original pen and watercolor sketches were engraved by Charles Michel Geoffroy. Professional colorists later hand tinted the plates. The coloring in most copies is relatively restrained, which lends the prints a delicate quality. In each engraving, Grandville's flower ladies are placed in appropriate settings, and their behavior sometimes reflects biological aspects of the flowers or their social symbolism.

In the illustration pictured on the facing page, a woman adorned with dahlia flowers sits at a table in an elegant and formal pose. She is seen in profile and presents a sophisticated aspect. In Rabin's entry for the dahlia he explains how the character of this flower lady relates to the dahlia's place in the gardening world. An excerpt from the 1847 English translation of the book by N. Cleaveland reads:

> *The Dahlia is a striking example of the influences of cultivation. Compare the flat meager original of this plant with the rich full glowing hemispheres of petals that, in all their thousand varieties of form and shade, adorn so many gardens.* (Rabin in Grandville, *The Flowers Personified*, vol. 2, 114)

Grandville del.   Ch. Geoffroy sc.

DAHLIA

G. de GONET Editeur

The attitude of Grandville's *Dahlia* is appropriately "cultivated" as she sits in an artfully decorated ironwork chair and gracefully lifts a flower. Her ladylike nature reflects the nineteenth-century perception that the dahlia was a "refined" flower.

    Les Fleurs animées was issued in installments to subscribers who paid for the book incrementally, a distribution technique that the French borrowed from the English in the nineteenth century. The book was originally published in eighty-three installments and cost twenty-five francs unbound. The Ellis Library example comes from the second publication of the book, which was distributed in a two-volume, ready-bound issue in 1847. The blind-stamped, polychrome and gilt cover design repeats the composition of the book's frontispiece. The beauty and complexity of the covers give the volumes a precious quality that would have attracted buyers and appealed to the Romantic tastes of nineteenth-century consumers. Indeed, *Les Fleurs animées* was a resounding success. It was issued in multiple editions and translated into English and German within a few years of its first publication.

JS

REFERENCES

Gottfried, Sello. *Grandville. Das gesamte Werk.* 2 vols. Berlin: Henschelveri, 1970.

Grandville, J. J., and Taxile Delord. *The Flowers Personified.* Translated by N. Cleaveland. New York: R. Martin, 1847.

Ray, Gordon. *The Art of the French Illustrated Book 1700 to 1914.* 2 vols. New York: The Pierpont Morgan Library and Cornell University Press, 1982.

Wick, Peter A. "Introduction," in *Les Fleurs animées: The Engraved Illustrations of J. J. Grandville.* New York: George Braziller, 1981.

REFERENCES
Alexander, Christine. *A Bibliography of the Manuscripts of Charlotte Brontë*. Westport, Conn.: Meckler Publishing and the Brontë Society, 1982.

——— . *The Early Writings of Charlotte Brontë*. New York: Prometheus, 1983.

——— , ed. *An Edition of the Early Writings of Charlotte Brontë*. Vol. II, part 1. Oxford: Shakespeare Head Press, 1991, 269–315.

——— , and Margaret Smith. *The Oxford Companion to the Brontës*. Oxford: Oxford University Press, 2003.

Brontë, Charlotte. *The Secret and Lily Hart: Two Tales*. Edited and transcribed by William Holz. Columbia: University of Missouri Press, 1978.

Christian, Mildred G. "A Census of Brontë Manuscripts in the United States: Part One." *Trollopian* 2, no. 3 (Dec. 1947): 190.

Ratchford, Fannie. *Legends of Angria: Compiled from the Early Writings of Charlotte Brontë*. New Haven: Yale University Press, 1933.

——— . *The Brontës' Web of Childhood*. New York: Russell & Russell, 1964.

Charlotte Brontë was born in Haworth, Yorkshire, England, in 1816. Along with her sisters Emily and Anne, Charlotte would one day become one of the most important novelists of the Victorian period. As children, the sisters and their brother Branwell cultivated their writing skills by developing long, imaginative sagas they called plays. The Brontës' plays eventually gave rise to a mythical land called Angria, which was peopled by characters the children created. Charlotte became the dominant artistic force behind the Angrian saga, and she and Branwell began to record their adventures as short stories with complex, interconnected plots.

The manuscript in the exhibition contains two installments of the saga: the short stories entitled *"The Secret"* and *"Lily Hart."* It consists of four sheets of notepaper folded into sixteen pages and originally sewn to make a booklet. The manuscript is dated November 27, 1833. Charlotte wrote the story in minuscule script and signed her name in cursive on the last page.

The diminutive size of the booklet and its script are characteristic of much of the Brontë juvenilia. The children may at first have written to the scale of their toys; a box of toy soldiers was the inspiration for the first of their plays, and their earliest manuscripts are the size of postage stamps. They may also have wished to emulate the look of published texts. One of Charlotte's school friends recalled that Charlotte and Branwell learned to write in tiny script "by writing in their magazine." They brought out a 'magazine' once a month, and wished it to look as much like print as possible (Alexander, *The Early Writings of Chcalotte Brontë*, 74). Although Charlotte and Branwell shared the world of Angria, they kept their plays closely guarded from outsiders, and the tiny handwriting may also have served to keep their world private and secret.

When Charlotte died in 1855, all of her personal papers and belongings were left to her husband, Arthur Nicholls. Nicholls sold the papers to the author Clement Shorter in 1895, and much of the juvenilia ended up in the possession of the book dealer T. J. Wise, who sold this manuscript in 1915. No information is available on the little booklet's whereabouts between 1915 and 1973, and it was presumed lost. However, the manuscript was rediscovered among the belongings of Evelyn Wadsworth Symington, wife of United States Senator Stuart Symington, after her death in 1973. Symington presented it to the University of Missouri Libraries in 1975.

When *"The Secret"* and *"Lily Hart"* were rediscovered, they filled holes in the Angrian storyline that had previously been left unexplained. *"The Secret"* focuses on Charlotte's heroine Marian Hume, the child bride of the dark, brooding and temperamental Marquis of Douro. Although Marian appears in many of the other stories *"The Secret"* contains surprising revelations about her past. By contrast, *"Lily Hart"* is a rags-to-riches romance and is the only story in which the title character appears. Since their discovery, both stories have been published twice and are available in *An Edition of the Early Writings of Charlotte Brontë* and *The Secret and Lily Hart: Two Tales*.

KBH

The book *Poems by Currer, Ellis, and Acton Bell* was the Brontë sisters' first published work. The publication grew out of the sisters' childhood plays and marks a dividing line between their juvenilia and their mature works.

While all four of the Brontë children participated in the Angrian play initially, Emily and Anne soon broke away from Charlotte and Branwell and formed their own fantasy world, an island called Gondal. Emily saw the siblings' epic worlds as intensely personal and did not share her writings with the rest of the family. Nevertheless, in 1845 Charlotte found and read a notebook containing Emily's Gondal poems.

> I looked it over, and something more than surprise seized me,—a deep conviction that these were not common effusions, nor at all like the poetry women generally write. I thought them condensed and terse, vigorous and genuine. To my ear, they had also a peculiar music—wild, melancholy, and elevating (Charlotte Brontë, cited in Barker, 478).

Impressed by her sister's talent, Charlotte approached Emily and suggested she publish her work. However, Emily, was not receptive to this idea; she had never shown her writing to anyone and was upset that Charlotte had read the poems without her consent. Perhaps to placate Emily, Anne showed Charlotte her own private Gondal poems as well, which Charlotte grudgingly judged to have "a sweet sincere pathos of their own" (Barker, 479). Despite Anne's efforts to smooth things over, it took hours for Emily to recover from the initial invasion of privacy. After much cajoling from Charlotte, Emily eventually gave in and agreed to allow publication of her poems (Barker, 478–479).

The three sisters determined to publish their poetry as a collection, and Emily consented to the plan as long as the sisters used pseudonyms and kept their project secret from family and friends. Drawing from the writings of the previous five years, Emily and Anne each contributed twenty-one poems, most of which related to their Gondal sagas, and Charlotte contributed nineteen she had written years earlier as part of her Angrian chronicles. According to Emily's wishes, all references to the authors' imaginary worlds were removed.

In 1846 Charlotte arranged for the poems to be published at the sisters' own considerable expense by Aylott and Jones of London. Of the initial 1,000-copy press run, fewer than 100 sold in the first two years. The book was a commercial failure and attracted little critical attention, but the few reviews it received were favorable enough to encourage the Brontës in their efforts. Within a year of the publication of *Poems*, Emily's *Wuthering Heights* and Anne's *Agnes Grey* were accepted by the publisher Thomas Cautley Newby, although they were not printed until much later. Charlotte's first novel was rejected, but her second, *Jane Eyre*, was published in late 1847. Although the first edition of *Poems* sold dismally, the sisters' subsequent literary successes were enough to produce a reissue in 1848.

Interest in the Brontës spread abroad as well. The volume of *Poems* in the exhibition is dated 1848, just a few months after the first publication of *Jane Eyre*, and is from the first edition printed in the United States. The title page bills each of the "Bells" as a newly published novelist.

KBH

POEMS

BY

CURRER, ELLIS, AND ACTON
BELL.

AUTHORS OF

"JANE EYRE," "WUTHERING HEIGHTS," "TENANT
OF WILDFELL HALL," ETC.

PHILADELPHIA:
LEA AND BLANCHARD.
1848.

CATALOGUE 29
Charlotte Brontë
(British, 1816–1855)
Emily Brontë
(British, 1818–1848) and
Anne Brontë
(British, 1820–1849)
Poems by Currer, Ellis, and
Acton Bell
(Frontispiece, pictured)
Printed text
Special Collections, Ellis Library
University of Missouri-Columbia

MEASUREMENTS
20 x 13.3 centimeters (cover)

REFERENCES
Alexander, Christine, and Margaret Smith. *The Oxford Companion to the Brontës.* Oxford: Oxford University Press, 2003.

Barker, Juliet. *The Brontës.* New York: St. Martin's Press, 1994.

Crump, R. W. *Charlotte and Emily Brontë, 1846–1915: A Reference Guide.* Boston: G. K. Hall, 1982.

Hargreaves, G. D. "The Publishing of *Poems* by Currer, Ellis and Acton Bell." *Brontë Society Transactions* 15 (1969): 294–300.

Passel, Anne. *Charlotte and Emily Brontë: An Annotated Bibliography.* New York: Garland, 1979.

CATALOGUE 30
*William Shakespeare
(English, 1564–1616),
Edited by Frederick S. Ellis
(English, 1830–1901)*
**The Poems of William
Shakespeare: Printed after
the Original Copies of Venus
and Adonis, 1593; The Rape
of Lucrece, 1594; Sonnets, 1609;
The Lover's Complaint, 1893**
*(Page 127, pictured)
Printed text with woodcuts
Special Collections, Ellis Library
University of Missouri-Columbia*

MEASUREMENTS
19.9 x 14.6 centimeters (cover)

As a result of new technology brought about by the Industrial Revolution, publishers were able to produce books inexpensively in large quantities, thereby reaching a broader audience and increasing profits. However, these mass-produced texts lacked the individuality and aesthetic qualities of earlier books. This led some publishing companies to begin printing old-fashioned, luxurious books in limited editions. Some of these books were printed on animal skin parchment in imitation of early Renaissance printed texts. Others were printed on high-grade rag paper.

The most renowned publishing company that produced these books was Kelmscott Press. William Morris, a leader of the Arts and Crafts movement, conceived and directed this press, which published *The Poems of William Shakespeare* pictured above.

Morris was an English socialist, architect, artist, designer, illuminator and typographer who profoundly influenced the Arts and Crafts movement and English Romanticism. He was born into a wealthy family, and during his education at Marlborough College and Oxford University, he became influenced by John Ruskin (1819–1900). He also established several enduring friendships with Dante Gabriel Rossetti (1828–1882), Edward Burne-Jones (1833–1898), Ford Madox Brown (1821–1893) and Philip Webb (1831–1915). Together, these men formed the Pre-Raphaelite Brotherhood. Believing that no hierarchy of artistic media should exist, the Pre-Raphaelites sought to raise the status of fine craftsmen. Morris applied this philosophy to book production when he established the Kelmscott Press. From 1891 to 1898, the press published a total of fifty-three books. Morris invented several type forms used at the Kelmscott Press: the Chaucer type, the Troy type and the Golden type. All of these fonts were based on letter forms used during the fourteenth, fifteenth and sixteenth centuries.

The Poems of William Shakespeare is typical of books published by the Kelmscott Press. Five hundred paper copies and ten vellum copies of the book were issued beginning on February 13, 1893. The text is printed slightly off-center in Golden type recalling decorative motifs of the sixteenth century, woodcuts of swirling vines topped with flowers frame the text.

SC

REFERENCES
Naylor, Gillian. *The Arts and Crafts Movement*. London: Sudio Vista Publishers, 1971.

Peterson, William. *A Bibliography of the Kelmscott Press*. Oxford: Clarendon Press, 1984.

Thompson, Susan Otis. *American Book Design and William Morris*. London: Oak Knoll Press and The British Library, 1977. Reprint, 1996.

William Morris and the Art of the Book. Oxford: Oxford University Press; The Pierpont Morgan Library, 1976.

CATALOGUE 31
*Sir Thomas Mallory
(English, ca. 1405–1471) and
Aubrey Vincent Beardsley
(British 1872–1898)*
Le Morte d'Arthur, *1909
(Chapter 9, page 614,
introductory illustration and*
**How Guenever Made Her a
Nun,** *pictured)
First Beardsley edition, 1893
Original text written ca. 1470
Printed text with line block
prints and two photogravure
frontispieces
Special Collections, Ellis Library
University of Missouri-Columbia*

MEASUREMENTS
26 x 21.5 centimeters (cover)

T he English author Sir Thomas Mallory retold the medieval legends associated with King Arthur in a single unified text titled *Le Morte d'Arthur*, written in 1470. At the end of the nineteenth century, the revived interest in all things medieval among artists and intellectuals ensured the popularity of a new illustrated edition of *Le Morte d'Arthur* that was published by Joseph M. Dent. The extended title of the book summarizes its contents: "The birth, life and acts of King Arthur, of his noble Knights of the Round Table, their marvelous enquests (sic) and adventures, the achieving of the San Greal and in the end le morte d'arthur with the delourous death and departing out of this world of them all."

Joseph Malaby Dent (1849–1926) was a British publisher who was aware of the fine books produced by William Morris' Kelmscott Press and other Arts and Crafts publishers. Unlike Morris, Dent was interested in creating high-quality, beautifully illustrated books with modern mechanical techniques. In 1822 he hired the twenty-year-old Aubrey Beardsley to illustrate his new deluxe edition which was based on Caxton's 1485 printing of the story. Like Morris' publications, Dent's book was conceived as an aesthetic object; its text and illustrations were integrated to produce a beautiful whole. Aside from the twenty-two large illustrations (see Cat. 32), Beardsley created the book's ornamental borders, historiated initials, headpieces, in-text decorations and binding covers. While Morris' type was hand set and his ilustrations were original woodcuts, Dent employed new printing technologies.

Beardsley's illustrations were made using a new photomechanical technique called line block (or line cut) printing. The printmaker began by photographing Beardsley's original pen and ink drawings onto zinc plates that were coated with light-sensitive gelatin. Once exposed to light, negative images of the drawings were sensitized, and the unsensitized gelatin was washed off the plate. The sensitized areas were then covered with acid-resistant wax resin, and the unsensitized areas were etched so that the original line drawings appeared in relief. The zinc matrices functioned like woodblocks, and the resulting prints resembled woodcuts. Line blocks are not hand carved, so they tend to exhibit freer, more organic lines and contours than do woodcuts.

Dent originally issued the books to subscribers in twelve parts between 1893 and 1894. Three hundred copies were printed in red and black on handmade paper while another 1,500 copies printed in black were issued in a smaller format on smooth, machine-made sheets. Subscribers who received the book in installments could pay Dent to have their loose sheets bound in tooled, gilt-leather covers designed by Beardsley. Ready-bound versions of the black and white edition were also made available.

The copy of *Le Mort d'Arthur* pictured above comes from the second edition published by Dent in 1909. This edition was published in a single volume (the first edition appeared in two volumes) and was limited to 1,000 copies that were distributed in England and 500 copies that were distributed in America.

JS

REFERENCES
Houfe, Simon. *The Dictionary of 19th Century British Book Illustrators*. Suffolk: Antique Collector's Club Ltd., 1998.

Macfall, Haldane. *Aubrey Beardsley: The Man and His Work*. London: John Lane The Bodley Head Limited, 1928.

Sturgis, Matthew. *Aubrey Beardsley, A Biography*. London: HarperCollins Publishers, 1998.

CATALOGUE 32
Aubrey Vincent Beardsley
(British 1872–1898)
How Sir Lancelot was
known by Dame Elaine, *1893*
From Sir Thomas Mallory's **Le**
Morte d'Arthur, *1893*
Line block print
Museum of Art and Archaeology
University of Missouri-Columbia
Gift of Museum Associates
2005.33

MEASUREMENTS
23.5 x 38.5 centimeters (sheet)

Aubrey Beardsley was born in Brighton, England, to an upper-middle-class family in 1872. A sickly child, he was attracted to drawing at an early age and was considered a prodigy. For a brief period of time, he made a living as a clerk, and at the encouragement of Pre-Raphaelite painter Sir Edward Burne Jones, attended night classes at the Westminster School of Art. By the age of twenty he was working as an illustrator, and the high quality of his work convinced J.M. Dent to commission him to illustrate *Le Morte d'Arthur* (see Cat. 31). This publication established the artist's reputation, and Beardsley became internationally known for his decorative, somewhat decadent illustrations for the works of Oscar Wilde and others. In 1898 at the young age of twenty-five, he suffered a premature death from tuberculosis.

The character of Beardsley's illustrations for *Le Morte d'Arthur* was appropriately and distinctly English. Many writers and critics recognized the influence of the Pre-Raphaelites in Beardsley's figures and ornamental designs. The Pre-Raphaelites had initiated an original "English" school of painting that was praised and recognized throughout Europe during the second half of the nighteenth century. The young Beardsley particularly admired the Pre-Raphaelite painter Sir Edward Burne-Jones, and the latter's influence is continually present in *Le Morte d'Arthur*.

How Sir Lancelot was known by Dame Elaine is one of sixteen double-page illustrations in *Le Morte d'Arthur*. It pictures a scene from Mallory's tale in which Dame Elaine, the mother of Lancelot's illegitimate son Galahad, finds her former lover wounded and sleeping in a garden. Beardsley captured the romantic tension of the episode in the space between the pages that physically separates Elaine from her ladies. She kneels next to Lancelot, her right hand touching his side and their heads close together. The path behind them may symbolically allude to the spiritual and physical journey both protagonists have experienced in order to meet again.

The print exhibits Beardsley's distinctively graphic manner as well as his decorative use of organic, curvilinear forms. Beardsley was a leading exponent of what was known in the nineteenth century as the "modern style," a term used to describe the *art nouveau* movement in Britain, and his simple contour drawings punctuated by expansive areas of black influenced many twentieth century illustrators.

JS

REFERENCES
Desmarais, Jane Haville. *The Beardsley Industry: The Critical Reception in England and France 1893–1914*. Aldershot: Ashgate Press, 1998.

Fletcher, Ian. *Aubrey Beardsley*. Boston: Twayne Publishers, 1987.

Macfall, Haldane. *Aubrey Beardsley: The Man and His Work*. London: John Lane The Bodley Head Limited, 1928.

CATALOGUE 33
William Shakespeare
(British, 1564–1616)
Nestore Leoni
(Italian, 1862–ca. 1940)
Shakespeare's Sonnets
2 volumes, 1901
(Cover and Frontispiece for
volume one, pictured)
Ink and pigments on vellum with
tooled leather bindings
Special Collections, Ellis Library
University of Missouri-Columbia
Gift of Mary Tisdale in memory of
Kenneth Tisdale

MEASUREMENTS
26 x 21 centimeters (cover)

REFERENCES
Arts and Crafts Essays.
London: Rivington, Percival,
& Company, 1893. Reprint,
1996.

Benton, Megan. *Beauty and the
Book: Fine Editions and Cultural
Distinction in America.* New
Haven: Yale University Press,
2000.

de Hamel, Christopher.
*The British Library Guide
to Manuscript Illumination:
History and Techniques.*
London: University of
Toronto Press, 2001.

Hindman, Sarah, and Nina
Rowe, eds. *Manuscript
Illumination in the Modern
Ages: Recovery and
Reconstruction.* Evanston,
Ill.: Mary and Leigh Block
Museum of Art, 2001.

Naylor, Gillian. *The Arts and
Crafts Movement.* London:
Studio Vista Publishers, 1971.

During the late nineteenth century, the Arts and Crafts movement in England spread throughout Europe and America in response to the mechanized production of material goods that was prompted by industrialization. Leaders of the movement, such as John Ruskin and William Morris, promoted quality craftsmanship and individually made handcrafted goods. By reviving past methods of production, they also hoped to renew preindustrial cultural values. Artists of the movement often found inspiration in medieval and Renaissance aesthetics and construction methods for architecture, furniture, textiles, jewelry and books. During this time, hand-decorated, luxurious books by celebrated authors were printed on parchment in limited editions and were purchased primarily by bibliophiles.

The George D. Sproul Company, located in New York and London, published the two volumes of sonnets by William Shakespeare that are displayed in this exhibition. Only eighteen copies were made available in America, and only twelve were sold in Europe. The publisher and the illuminator, Nestore Leoni, both signed the copy pictured above. The Sproul-Leoni Shakespeare represents a return to medieval and Renaissance practices of producing fine printed books characterized by the use of spacious margins, vellum or fine paper and illuminations to decorate the pages and enhance the text.

Manuscripts and finely printed books were a collaborative effort of specialized artisans during the medieval and Renaissance periods. The process of creation encompassed several different stages, and this process was used to make *Shakespeare's Sonnets*. First, an expensive form of parchment called vellum was made from animal skin that had been soaked in a lime bath, stretched on a frame to dry and cut into pages. The text was then copied by hand or printed onto the pages, and illuminators added decorations and pictures. Finally, the book was bound and a cover added to complete the process. The style of the illuminations in *Shakespeare's Sonnets* most closely resembles those of sixteenth-century French manuscripts and early printed books, which were characterized by the use of vivid colors, swirling vines, acanthus leaves and abundant gold leafing. The illuminations, however, combine common elements from the medieval and Renaissance styles of several different European countries, so the final result is a distinctly modern hybrid of earlier styles.

SC

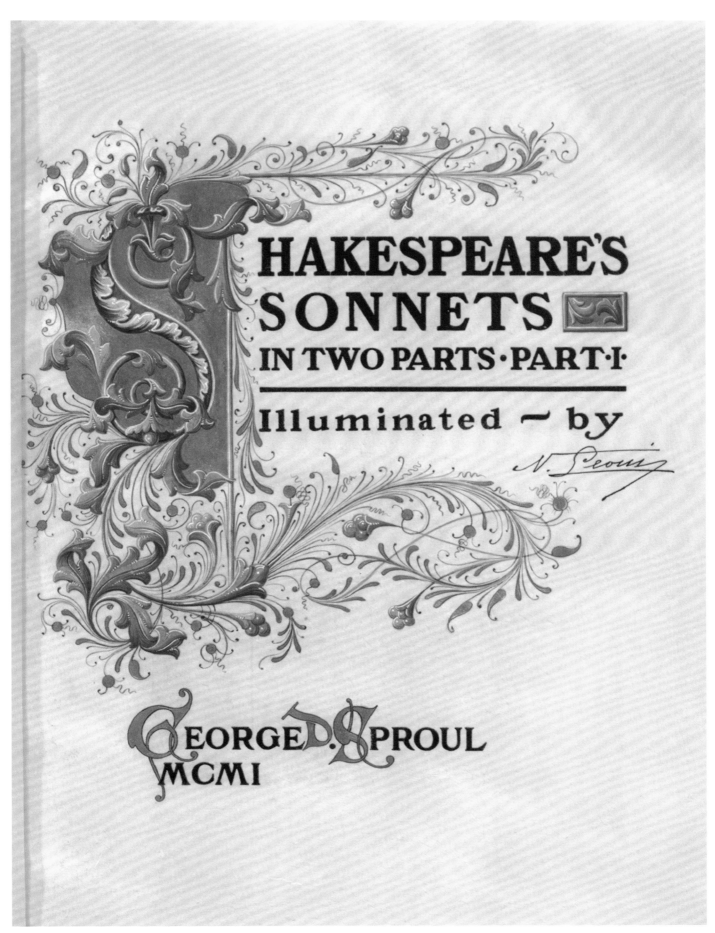

SHAKESPEARE'S
SONNETS
IN TWO PARTS · PART · I ·

Illuminated ～ by

GEORGE D. SPROUL
MCMI

CATALOGUE 34
Frederick Oakes Sylvester
(American, 1869–1915)
***The Great River**, 1911*
(Cover and watercolor
frontispiece, pictured)
Printed text with photomechanical
reproductions and an original
watercolor frontispiece
The State Historical Society
of Missouri

MEASUREMENTS
10.16 x 6.35 centimeters (cover)

Frederick Oakes Sylvester was born in Brockton, Mass., in 1869. In 1891 he moved to New Orleans to become director of the Art Department of Newcomb College.

In New Orleans he first encountered the Mississippi River and took special interest in its levee and bustling industry. By the time he moved to St. Louis one year later to teach art at Central High School and at The Principia in Illinois, he was enamored with the river. While living in St. Louis, he painted numerous images of the Mississippi that concentrated on the industrial riverfront activities and Eads Bridge. Although Sylvester's appreciation of the waterway began in New Orleans, his personal attachment intensified after moving to the Midwest where he used the great

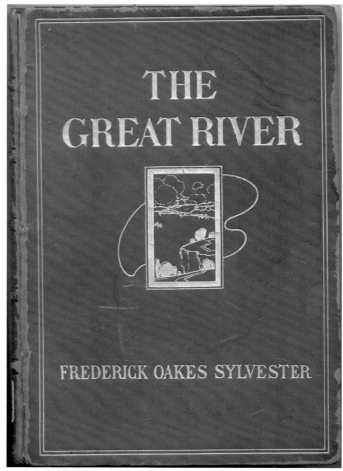

Cover

river almost exclusively as the subject of his artwork. Because of Sylvester's emotional and spiritual reaction to the natural world around him, he has been described as a transcendental regionalist or realistic impressionist. But his intensely personal work does not easily fit within conventional artistic movements.

In his early Missouri paintings, Sylvester often represented the relationship between man and his modern, industrial use of the waterway as harmonious and natural. In 1902 Sylvester bought a home in Elsah, Illinois, a small town on the bluffs of the Mississippi. There, Sylvester abandoned his earlier interest in industrial river life and used the river landscape, bluffs and palisades in his paintings to express his intimate relationship with nature. Deeply spiritual and religious, Sylvester's art reflected his belief that the ways of the river held deeper meaning.

In 1911 the artist published a book titled *The Great River*, a personal and romantic collection of poems accompanied by images that reflected his spiritual connection with the Mississippi. Each book was an original edition and contained a unique, signed watercolor by Sylvester. The book in this exhibition is an Edition de Luxe. This publication was limited to 100 copies. The *Untitled Landscape* in Cat. 35 is one of the 100 original watercolors that served as frontispieces for the book. Inside *The Great River*, black and white photographs accompanied each poem. The original photographs were copied onto the pages using the photogravure process, a photomechanical printing technique invented by Karl Klic of Vienna in 1879. To make photogravure prints, copperplates grained with resin dust are etched through gelatin relief images that have been prepared photographically. The technique was used extensively by pictorial photographers at the end of the nineteenth century and was well-suited to Sylvester's elegiac landscapes. The combination of original watercolor images and modern photomechanical reproductions reflected Sylvester's view of

Watercolor Frontispiece

man's place in the natural world. The artist did not see nature and technology at odds but believed that man and his inventions could exist in harmony with nature.

The title poem describes a personified river whose course mirrors the life cycle of man. The river is born in the hills, falls in love with the sky and finally encounters eternity as it meets the sea, just as man is born, marries and reunites with the divine at death. Sylvester's images and poems during this period reflect his view of the river as an eternal entity, a witness to the history of the world and man's endeavors. Innocent and eternal, the river approaches the divine.

In New Orleans Sylvester acquired technical proficiency and adopted the main tenets of the Arts and Crafts Movement that stressed the unity of art and life. During the early 1900s, his art reflected the influence of nineteenth-century luminist and tonalist painters. The artist was also influenced by the paintings of the Hudson River School, which emphasized the presence of God in nature. The watercolors included in *The Great River* are impressionistic and serene; they are strictly landscapes with few human figures. In the example included here, the sky and water are painted a vivid blue while the trees and landscape are portrayed with more subdued browns and greens. The landscape is lit by indirect, soft sunlight. Like many compositions in *The Great River,* a twisting, unpaved path leads the viewer into the landscape beyond, which is framed by trees and natural elements.

EWA

REFERENCES

Collester, Jeanne Colette. *Frederick Oakes Sylvester: The Principia Collection*. St. Louis: Principia Corp., 1988.

Crouther, Betty J. "Deciphering the Mississippi River Iconography of Frederick Oakes Sylvester," *Muse* 20 (1986): 81–89.

Williams, Paul O. *Frederick Oakes Sylvester: the Artist's Encounter with Elsah.* Elsah, Ill.: Historic Elsah Foundation, 1986.

CATALOGUE 35

Thomas Hart Benton
(American, 1889–1975)
It was a Steamboat that
Killed Herself on a Rock, *1942*
From **The Adventures of**
Huckleberry Finn *by Mark*
Twain (Samuel Clemens)
(American, 1835–1910)
Wash drawing
The State Historical Society
of Missouri
Gift of Thomas Hart Benton
66–0025

MEASUREMENTS

23.81 x 15.24 centimeters (image)

REFERENCES

Thomas Hart Benton's
Illustrations from Mark Twain:
The Adventures of Tom Sawyer,
The Adventures of Huckleberry
Finn, and Life on the Mississippi
from The State from The State
Historical Society of Missouri
Collection. Columbia,
Missouri: Mid-America Arts
Alliance, 1976.

Twain, Mark. *The Adventures*
of Huckleberry Finn. Illustrated
by Thomas Hart Benton. New
York: The Limited Editions
Club, 1942.

This edition of *The Adventures of Huckleberry Finn*, written by Mark Twain (Samuel Clemens) and illustrated by Thomas Hart Benton, was published in 1942 by the Limited Editions Club. Founded in 1929 by George Macy, this club offered finely crafted, illustrated editions of literary classics through subscriptions. Each of the 1,500 subscribers received twelve books over the course of one year. Advertising campaigns attracted subscribers by marketing the books as investments that would increase in value over time.

Twain's *The Adventures of Huckleberry Finn* was first published in 1884 and is considered to be one of the foremost classics in American literature. Written in the vernacular from the point of view of Huckleberry Finn, an uneducated boy from Missouri, the tale tells the story of the adventures of Huck and the runaway slave Jim as they travel down the Mississippi on a raft. The informal, conversational writing style is both humorous and poignant capturing the ephemeral moments of everyday life. Thomas Hart Benton's lively Regionalist style was particularly well-suited to represent episodes from this epic tale written in colloquial prose. Both Twain and Benton found their main sources of inspiration in rural areas of America, and both rebelled against the general cultural trends of their respective eras. Twain rejected, and sometimes mocked, the Romantic, poetic writing style that was fashionable during the nineteenth century. He chose instead to present his stories from the personal perspectives of ordinary and often marginalized people. Likewise, after experimenting with abstract and nonrepresentational art, Thomas Hart Benton denounced the elitism of Modernism and developed a representational style that celebrated the often ignored people of rural America.

Although some books published by Limited Editions Club contained original etchings and lithographs, The *Adventures of Huckleberry Finn* was illustrated with fine quality photographic reproductions of Benton's sepia-toned pen, ink and wash drawings (the artist eventually donated all these drawings to The State Historical Society of Missouri). Benton explained his approach to illustration at the beginning of the book in the essay "A Note by the Illustrator." He wrote that he admired Edward Windsor Kemble's 1884 illustrations for the first edition of Twain's classic because they were not too literal. Benton said, "He knew that story pictures and book pictures in particular should be on the order of visual stimulants rather than positive depictions. He had the artist's sense of appropriateness." Benton attempted to emulate this quality in his own illustrations, which he based on hundreds of drawings he had made during a trip to the "backwaters of the great rivers" in Virginia, the Carolinas, Tennessee and Kentucky.

The wash drawing *It was a steamboat that had killed herself on a rock* illustrates Chapter 12, "Better Let Blame Well Alone." In this chapter, Huck and Jim spot a sinking steamboat during a storm and climb aboard. After a short time, Jim heads back to the raft, but Huck remains on board and overhears two men planning to kill a third man by leaving him on the sinking vessel to drown. In Benton's drawing, a lightning bolt illuminates the night sky as Huck and Jim approach the sinking boat. The composition is organized around a series of dynamic diagonals that create an off-kilter, uneasy mood. Benton's characteristic undulating forms and dramatic chiaroscuro also create drama and reflect the emotional energy of Twain's prose.

SC

CATALOGUE 36
Thomas Hart Benton
(American, 1889–1975)
Here a Captive Heart Busted,
Chapter Heading for Chapter 38,
*1942, From **The Adventures***
***of Huckleberry Finn** by Mark*
Twain (Samuel Clemens)
Wash drawing
The State Historical Society
of Missouri
Gift of Thomas Hart Benton

MEASUREMENTS
8.57 x 16.19 centiments (image)

The first edition of Mark Twain's *The Adventures of Huckleberry Finn*, which is set before the Civil War, was published in 1884 shortly after the Reconstruction period that followed the war. The book deals with themes of slavery, escape, freedom, family life and friendship. Huck Finn, the innocent young protagonist who is Tom Sawyer's closest friend, leaves his home to avoid his abusive, racist, alcoholic father. He joins an escaped slave, Jim, who was separated from his wife and children and is attempting to flee to the free state of Ohio. Together, the two float down the Mississippi River on a raft and encounter murderers, thieves, hypocrites and also helpful, caring people along the way. During their journey, they form a close friendship that challenges Huck's former prejudiced beliefs about American blacks.

Twain's daring, brash book combines humor and social commentary. His use of vernacular language and his approach to Jim's character confronted issues of class and race in ways that were unprecedented in the nineteenth century. Consequently, controversy immediately developed when the first edition was released. Today, the book continues to spark debate and dialogue among academicians, teachers, parents and young people about matters of race and book censorship in schools.

Thomas Hart Benton's 1942 illustrations for *The Adventures of Huckleberry Finn* exhibit some stereotypical depictions of African Americans that are no longer accepted, such as Jim's wide-eyed, open-mouthed expression in this illustration. The picture illustrates a scene from Chapter 38, "Here a Captive Heart Busted." In the previous chapters, Jim had been captured and chained in slave quarters. Tom and Huck had devised a plan to rescue him, and Benton's illustration shows Tom convincing Jim that before his escape he must write an inscription on the wall where he is imprisoned. Because Jim is illiterate, Tom writes the "mournful inscription" for him. He includes the following numbered sentences:

1. *Here a captive heart busted.*
2. *Here a poor prisoner forsook by the world and friends, fretted out his sorrowful life.*
3. *Here a lonely heart broke, and a worn spirit went to its rest, after thirty-seven years of solitary captivity.*
4. *Here, homeless and friendless, after thirty-seven years of bitter captivity, perished a noble stranger, natural son of Louis XIV.*

The sentences written by Tom mock nineteenth-century Romantic sentiment while Benton's energetic and expressive wash drawing captures the emotional interaction of the characters as well as the humorous implications of the scene.

SC

REFERENCES
Benton, Thomas Hart.
An Artist in America, 4th
ed. Columbia, Missouri:
University of Missouri Press,
1983.

Ward, Geoffrey C., and
Dayton Duncan. *Mark Twain*.
New York: Alfred A. Knopf,
2001.

CATALOGUE 37
Lynd Ward
(American, 1905–1985)
Wild Pilgrimage: A Novel in Woodcuts, 1932
(Fantasy image of lovers, thirty-second illustration in the novel, pictured)
Wood engravings
Special Collections, Ellis Library University of Missouri-Columbia

MEASUREMENTS
25 x 18 centimeters (cover)

REFERENCES
Beronä, David. "Picture Stories: Erick Drooker and the Tradition of Woodcut Novels." *Print Quarterly* 20, no. 1 (March 2003): 61–73.

McCausland, Elizabeth, ed. *Work for Artists: What? Where? How?* New York: American Artists Group Inc, 1947.

Ward, Lynd. *Storyteller without Words: The Wood Engravings of Lynd Ward.* New York: Harry N. Abrams Inc, 1974.

Willett, Perry. *The Silent Shout: Frans Masereel, Lynd Ward, and the Novel in Woodcuts.* Bloomington: Indiana University Libraries, 1997.

In the 1920s and 1930s, illustrated books without words became fashionable. The trend was initiated by well-known German printmakers such as Karl Schmidt-Rottluff and Max Pechstein, who created small portfolios of wordless narratives told with sequential woodcuts. Later publishers adapted this form to the popular market, and photo reproductions eventually replaced original prints. In the popular press, these wordless books sometimes included written explanatory essays, which, according to historian Perry Willet, often interfered with their "silent aesthetic" messages.

Lynd Ward, the illustrator of *Wild Pilgrimage*, was born in Chicago to Harry F. Ward, a Methodist minister and founding member of the American Civil Liberties Union. Ward learned printmaking and book design at the National Academy of Graphic Arts in Leipzig, Germany, where he studied with the famous printmaker and book illustrator Hans Alexander Müller (1888–1962). In Leipzig, Ward discovered a book titled *Mein Studenbuch*, which was created by the Belgian engraver Franz Masereel (1889–1972). The book conveyed its storyline with illustrations alone, and Ward was inspired to create his first wordless book, 1929's *God's Man* (the first novel without words that was printed in the United States). Between 1929 and 1937, Ward published a total of five wordless novels, including *Wild Pilgrimage*, which was published in 1932. In this book, ninety-five reproductions of Ward's wood engravings relay the poignant story of a simple working man who is born into an industrialized world and is conscious of the vast differences between his external environment and the inner workings of his own mind. Ward differentiates between the two by alternating between black and red ink. Black and white images illustrate the man's societal experiences while red and white images represent his internal fantasies and desires.

As a member of the American League Against War and Fascism, Ward participated in leftist politics during the 1930s and 1940s. Although he was not a Communist, he criticized the American capitalist economic system and admired the socialism of the Soviet Union. Ward's progressive political views are reflected in *Wild Pilgrimage.* The protagonist becomes weary of industrialization, capitalism and the exploitative practices of manufacturing entrepreneurs. As a result, the character decides to leave the city and seek an uncomplicated life in a rural setting. A farmer provides him with work, but when he witnesses a lynching, the protagonist discovers that rural life can be tainted with violence and racism.

After viewing the lynching, Ward's central character escapes into a world of fantasy. The color scheme of the book shifts from black and white to red and white when the man imagines that he is having a romantic affair with his employer's wife. The illustration on the facing page represents this fantasy. The color scheme returns to black and white when the central character attempts to act on his romantic and erotic thoughts. The wife rejects his inappropriate advances, and an angry mob chases him away. He eventually finds shelter and contentment with another man who tries to help him overcome his despair. But this comfortable life is interrupted when the protagonist dreams of an uprising in the factories in which he previously worked. He leaves the farm and returns to the city where he joins a strike and attempts to protest injustices brought on by industrialization. The protagonist's protest is cut short when he is killed by the police, who leave his body in the street.

SC

CATALOGUE 38
Rockwell Kent
(American 1882–1971)
Beowulf, 1931
Lithograph
Anonymous loan

MEASUREMENTS
48 x 39 centimeters (sheet)

Rockwell Kent was a renowned painter and printmaker who became one of America's finest and most inventive illustrators. Influenced by British printmakers, American social realists and international art deco designers, he developed a distinctively spare and controlled style. Politically he was a controversial figure. He contributed illustrations to the left-wing journal *The Masses* and eventually bequeathed his personal painting collection to the people of the Soviet Union.

In 1930, Kent became a nationally known illustrator after Lakeside Press of Chicago issued a limited edition of Herman Melville's *Moby Dick* that was illustrated with reproductions of Kent's strikingly graphic pen and ink drawings. This publication contributed to the revival of interest in Melville and established Kent's reputation as a great interpreter of literature. Kent also helped revive the Arts and Crafts movement's tradition of designing books as coherent aesthetic objects with the artist determining the layout, typeface, binding and other visual aspects.

In 1932 Kent designed and illustrated a new edition of the medieval saga *Beowulf* that had been translated from the Old English by William Ellery Leonard. The book was published by Pynson Printers, a New York press founded in 1922 by Elmer Adler. Pynson Printers specialized in finely crafted books, and the text of *Beowulf* was typeset by hand. The first edition was limited to 950 copies, each of which was signed and numbered by Kent, who also made a thumbprint impression in each book.

The artist originally drew his illustrations for *Beowulf* on lithographic limestones, and proofs of each image were pulled and transferred onto zinc plates. Nine hundred and fifty impressions from each of these plates were then printed by the offset process. The image on the facing page comes from an initial printing of the original lithograph that was issued independently in 1931 in an edition of 150. It is a mirror image of the zinc-plate print illustrated in the 1932 Pynson Printers edition. The lithograph pictures Beowulf victorious over Grendel, a monster that had tormented and murdered the subjects of King Hrothgar. Beowulf fought Grendel barehanded, and the hero's iron grip allowed him to rip the monster's arm from its socket. Although the creature escaped, it eventually died in its underwater lair. Kent pictures the dramatic horror of the episode by showing Beowulf as a powerful nude figure grasping Grendel's severed arm. The grain of the litho stone is clearly visible under the drawing, and its stony pattern imparts a sculptural quality to the statuesque monumentality of the figure.

JS

REFERENCES
Adler, Elmer. "The Making of a Book." *The Dolphin* 2 (1935): 144–153.

Jones, Dan Burne. "Books Illustrated by Rockwell Kent." *American Book Collector* 14 (1964): 43–50.

Barnett   Rockwell Kent

CATALOGUE 39
Peggy Bacon
(American, 1895–1987)
The Haunted House, *1959*
Etching
Museum of Art and Archaeology
University of Missouri-Columbia
Purchased by John Pickard
X–82

MEASUREMENTS
29.1 x 20.5 centimeters (sheet)

REFERENCES
"Peggy Bacon, Kindly Humorist, Has a Show." *The Art Digest* 8 (March 1, 1934): 8.

"Peggy Bacon–Who Laughs at Life." *The Art Digest* 11, 12 (May 1, 1937): 9.

Robinson, Tom. *Buttons.* New York: The Viking Press, 1938. Reprint, 1966.

Tarbell, Roberta. *Peggy Bacon: Personalities and Places.* Washington, D.C.: National Collection of Fine Arts, Smithsonian Institution Press, 1975.

Tucker, Nicholas. *The Child and the Book: A Psychological and Literary Exploration.* London: Cambridge University Press, 1981.

Born in Ridgefield, Conn., Peggy Bacon began to illustrate poems in letters to her family at the age of seven. Her father, a landscape painter, and her mother, a miniature painter, both studied at the Art Students League in New York City, where Bacon later attended classes taught by Kenneth Hayes Miller, John Sloan and George Bellows. During her five years at the Art Students League, Bacon began to produce artwork with the wit and frankness of Sloan and the honesty of Miller. Her paintings, drawings and illustrations reveal her sharp wit and are often humorous. She was interested in depicting people and animals within realistic settings, and often included cats in her compositions.

The Haunted House is an etching that Bacon made in 1959 after a pastel drawing that she had created to illustrate *Buttons*, a children's book written by Tom Robinson and published in 1938. *Buttons* is a picture book that contains fifty of Bacon's illustrations. The book relays the story of a tough alley cat. Born in an ash can, the cat must scrounge and fight for food, and eventually he becomes "King of the Alley" with ragged fur, torn ears and a broken tail. One day, the cat becomes stuck in a tree while chasing another cat, and when a fireman attempts to rescue him, he jumps through the window of a nearby house. He wanders around the house and falls asleep in an ash can in the basement. A little girl who lives in the house feeds him, keeps him inside and names him Buttons. In the end, Buttons is restored to health and forgets he was ever an alley cat; instead, he is a "gentleman" with soft fur, a straight tail and healed legs and ears. Bacon's etching, *The Haunted House*, depicts the alley cat as he descends the stairs to the basement during his exploration of the house. The story reflects the atmosphere within the United States during the Depression years when many people became homeless and struggled to meet their basic needs. By obtaining a safe haven and nourishment, the cat becomes a gentleman. This chain of events may reflect the popular political idealogy of the period that called for government intervention to help the poor and needy.

Bacon's images of cats demonstrate a close observation of feline behavior, expressions and poses. Her original pastel drawings for *Buttons* were exhibited as a group in 1939 at the Rehn Gallery in New York. In response to the exhibition, Royal Cortissoz wrote:

> *Not for her the sleek and pampered Siamese or any of its lordly kin— but the yowling warrior of the backyard fence, the 'alley-cat' of sinister renown. Miss Bacon draws him to life and exposes his shreds of character with almost macabre realism.* (Cortissoz in Tarbell, 42)

Roberta Tarbell, author of *Peggy Bacon: Personality and Places*, commented that these portraits of a scraggly, scrawny street cat are some of Peggy Bacon's finest and most original works. Tarbell continued her praise by writing, "Fully confident in both her medium and her subject, she deftly depicted the salient character of some of Manhattan's toughest customers." Bacon's decision to make an etching from an original drawing for *Buttons* over twenty years later implies that she too cherished these illustrations of a scraggly feline.

SC

The Haunted House   Peggy Bacon

Modern and Contemporary Books

Joan Stack
Associate Curator

*Museum of Art and Archaeology
University of Missouri-Columbia*

In the first half of the twentieth century, a niche market developed for fine art books. By 1920 technology had revolutionized book production, and few original engravings or lithographs illustrated texts. However, some publishers realized that an elite group of art lovers would pay high prices for well-crafted, limited-edition books illustrated with original prints. The most famous of these publishers, Limited Editions Club in New York, invited the world's leading artists and book designers to produce special editions of literary classics. Although many of these editions were illustrated with high-quality photomechanical images, some contained original lithographs and etchings.

The twentieth century also saw the development of "artists' books." These books were originally conceived in the nineteenth century as beautifully crafted, but traditionally formatted books designed by artists. By the early twentieth century, however, minimalists, futurists, surrealists and Dadaists were creating books that reflected their aesthetic and philosophical ideas. This early experimentation challenged conventional notions about the very nature of the book.

By the 1960s, artists had reinvented the concept of the book. Influenced by conceptual, installation and performance art, they experimented with collage, appropriation, assemblage and mixed media. Some designed books as ephemeral objects that were meant to change or even disintegrate over time. Others conceived of their books as sculptural objects and encouraged viewers to appreciate their three-dimensionality and beautiful materials. Some artist's books are one-of a-kind productions while others are issued in small edition multiples. Some are constructed from durable, high-quality materials while others are deliberately crafted from the cheap, disposable "stuff" of the popular culture. In all cases, viewers participate in the creation of meaning for these books, as change, time and point-of-view are often essential aesthetic elements in their design.

In 1935 Henri Matisse produced six soft-ground etchings to illustrate an edition of *Ulysses* published by the Limited Editions Club. The book, by Irish author James Joyce, was first published in 1922. The novel takes place in a single day in twentieth-century Dublin, and its characters and episodes are based on Homer's *Odyssey*. Between 1922 and 1933, *Ulysses* was banned in the United States for obscenity, so this 1935 publication was one of the first editions available to the American public.

At the time of the 1935 publication, Matisse was one of the most celebrated artists in the world. He helped create what we understand today as twentieth-century "Modernism." He first gained recognition as a leader of the Fauve movement around 1905. Matisse was also a well-known printmaker who often focused his attention on simple linear contours.

Matisse based his six etchings for the 1935 edition of *Ulysses* on Homer's original story rather than on Joyce's modern tale. Both Matisse and Joyce interpreted Homer's epic in ways that reflected twentieth-century aesthetics—Matisse with his lines and Joyce with his words. Although scholars are unsure of whether Matisse thoroughly read *Ulysses*, he surely had sufficient enough experience with the book to produce these etchings. Matisse claimed that his plates were the products of his mind as he contemplated Joyce's book.

The Limited Editions Club released 1,500 copies of the 1935 edition. Each copy contained six original etchings by Matisse along with reproductions of his preliminary drawings. Matisse signed all 1,500 copies, and Joyce also signed 250 of these. Each signed copy of the edition is numbered, and the book in this exhibition is number 1,078.

The designer of the Limited Editions Club's publication of *Ulysses*, George Macy, described his experience with Matisse in this way:

> *I have never been more greatly impressed with the mental facility of an artist than when I suggested to Matisse that he should illustrate Ulysses. He said, over the telephone, that he had never read it. I got Stuart Gilbert to send him a copy of Mr. Gilbert's translation into French. The very next morning, Mr. Matisse reported that he had read the book, that he understood its eighteen episodes to be parodies of similar episodes in the Odyssey, that he would like to give point to this fact by making his illustrations actually illustrations of the original episodes of Homer! I may have been taken in, of course. If I was not, it can surely be said that Henri Matisse grasped this book quicker than any other man ever did.* (Macy, cited in Newman, item 71)

JK

CATALOGUE 40
James Joyce
(Irish, 1882–1941) and
Henri Matisse
(French, 1869–1954)
***Ulysses**, 1935 (text first*
published, 1922)
(Page 334, preliminary sketches
*and final etching for **Symbolic***
***Landscape, Ithaca**, pictured)*
Printed text with soft-ground
etchings and other photomechanical
illustrations
Special Collections, Ellis Library
University of Missouri-Columbia

MEASUREMENTS
30.4 x 23.5 centimeters (cover)

REFERENCES
Gross, Anthony. *Etching, Engraving, and Intaglio Printing*. London: Oxford University Press, 1973.

Guillaud, Jacqueline, and Maurice Guillaud. *Matisse: Rhythm and Line*. Paris: Guillaud Editions, 1987.

Newman, Ralph Geoffrey. *Great and Good Books: A Bibliographical Catalogue of the Limited Editions Club, 1929-1985*. Chicago: Ralph Geoffrey Newman Inc, 1989.

Turner, Caroline, and Roger Benjamin. *Matisse*. Australia: Queensland Art Gallery, 1995.

Preliminary Sketch #1

Preliminary Sketch #2

Final Etching

CATALOGUE 41–46
Henri Matisse
(French, 1869–1954)
Six prints illustrating James
Joyce's novel **Ulysses***, 1935*
Soft ground etchings
Museum of Art and Archaeology
University of Missouri-Columbia
Gift of Museum Associates
92.79.1–6

MEASUREMENTS
41.5 x 31.7 centimeters (sheets)

By 1935 Matisse had amassed a great deal of experience as a printmaker, but the prints for *Ulysses* (see Cat. 41) were his only use of soft-ground etching. Soft-ground etching is a technique in which the artist first prepares a metal plate by covering it with a soft-ground (a mixture of wax, bitumen, resin and grease or oil). The artist then lays a piece of textured paper atop the soft-ground and draws his or her design on the paper. When the drawing is complete, the artist lifts the paper from the plate. In the areas where pressure was applied, the ground is partially removed along with the paper. When the plate is etched, some of the ground remains in the drawn lines and gives prints made from this process the look of crayon drawings.

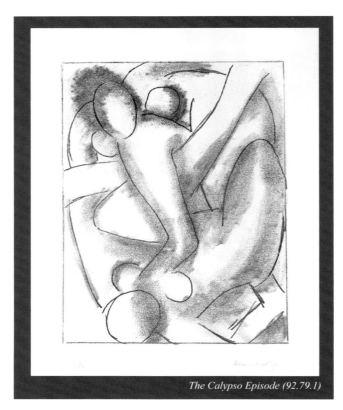

The Calypso Episode (92.79.1)

  Matisse began the etchings for *Ulysses* by making several preliminary sketches. Reproductions of these sketches are included in the Limited Editions Club book along with the final etchings. Compared with the final product, the figures in these sketches are more complex, and details such as faces and hair are more carefully articulated. Because of the numerous gestural lines, the sketches have a spontaneous, dynamic appearance and are full of emotion. With each drawing, Matisse simplified the forms and removed detail. The contours in the final etchings are reduced to only the essential lines.

JK

REFERENCES
Gross, Anthony. *Etching, Engraving, and Intaglio Printing.* London: Oxford University Press, 1973.

Guillaud, Jacqueline, and Maurice Guillaud. *Matisse: Rhythm and Line.* Paris:1` Guillaud Editions, 1987.

Newman, Ralph Geoffrey. *Great and Good Books: A Bibliographical Catalogue of the Limited Editions Club, 1929-1985.* Chicago: Ralph Geoffrey Newman Inc, 1989.

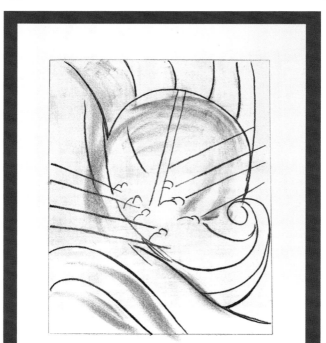

Aeolus, Cave of the Winds (92.79.2)

The Cyclops (92.79.3)

The Episode of Nausicaa (92.79.4)

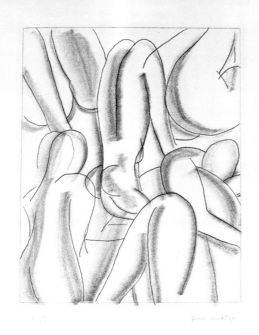

The Circe Episode (92.79.5)

Symbolic Landscape, Ithaca (92.79.6)

CATALOGUE 47
Gilbert Seldes
(1893–1970)
Aristophanes
(ca. 450–385 B.C.E)
Lysistrata, *1934*
(Page 115, **scene from the end**
of Lysistrata, *pictured)*
Illustrated by Pablo Picasso
(1881–1973)
Printed text with etchings and
photomechanical illustrations
Special Collections, Ellis Library
University of Missouri-Columbia

MEASUREMENTS
29.6 x 23.8 centimeters (cover)

*L*ysistrata is one of several Limited Editions Club books included in this catalogue. This book, illustrated by Pablo Picasso, reproduces a celebrated modern-English translation by Gilbert Seldes of the ancient Greek play. Seldes was born in 1893 in Alliance, New Jersey, and grew up on a Utopian farm colony with a father who encouraged him to read and collect books of value. Throughout his life, Seldes was an innovator in media. He edited, wrote and adapted many plays and prepared scripts for radio programs. He eventually became the first Director of Television for CBS and served as the founding dean of the Annenberg School of Communications in New York.

In 1930 Seldes translated and adapted *Lysistrata*, a drama written by the Athenian playwright Aristophanes (ca. 450–385 B.C.E). The play tells the story of Lysistrata, an Athenian woman, who convinced the females of Athens, Sparta and Thebes to withhold sexual favors from their men in order to bring about an end to the Peloponnesian War. In his introduction, Seldes explained that because Aristophanes did not sentimentalize or romanticize the themes of war, sex and love, audiences of the 1930s were able to relate to the story. Seldes compared Aristophanes with the Irish writer George Bernard Shaw (1856–1950). He claimed that both playwrights were cultural and social critics of their time. Seldes also argued that Aristophanes wrote satire with a deep moral fervor and that his naturalistic handling of the relationship between the sexes (often criticized by twentieth-century conservatives) should not be construed as lewd.

In his introduction, Seldes also argued that the Spanish artist Pablo Picasso was an ideal illustrator for this modern translation of *Lysistrata*. Picasso had become famous in the early years of the twentieth century as a leader of the avant-garde Cubist movement. By the 1930s, however, he was working in a modern "classical" style. Between 1930 and 1937, he completed nearly 100 etchings for the *Suite Vollard*. These prints are characterized by a spare, linear approach to form that recalls that of fifth-century Greek vase painters and Etruscan mirror engravers. Picasso's subject matter in the *Suite Vollard* was often erotic, and it was sometimes inspired by classical literature, especially the ancient story of the Minotaur.

Picasso's 1934 illustrations for Seldes' *Lysistrata* resemble his etchings for the *Suite Vollard*. The book includes both photomechanical images of Picasso's drawings and original etchings. The image illustrated here is an original etching that represents a scene from the end of the play. The Athenian Lykon and the Spartan envoy have agreed to settle their differences in order to have peace with the women from Athens and Sparta. The etching illustrates the beginning of Bacchanalian music, dancing, drinking and love making as the protagonists celebrate the fact "that the struggles are over and no more shall Greek raise sword against Greek."

SW

REFERENCES
Bolliger, Hans."Introduction,"
in *Picasso's Vollard Suite*.
Translated by Norbert
Guterman. New York: Harry
N. Abrams Inc, 1997.

Florman, Lisa. *Myth and
Metamorphosis: Picasso's
Classical Prints from the 1930s*.
Cambridge, Mass: The MIT
Press, 2000.

Kammen, Michael. *The Lively
Arts: Gilbert Seldes and the
Transformation of Cultural
Criticism in the United States*.
Oxford: Oxford University
Press, 1996.

CATALOGUE 48
Octavio Paz
(Mexican, 1914–1998)
***Three Poems**, 1987*
***(Red Samurai**, illustration for*
The Skin of the World, The
***Sound of the World**, pictured)*
Printed text with lithographs
Illustrated by Robert Motherwell
(American, 1915–1991)
Special Collections, Ellis Library
University of Missouri-Columbia

MEASUREMENTS
55 x 46 centimeters (cover)

REFERENCES
Bass, Ruth. "Matchmakers."
ArtNews (February, 1987):
9–10.

Caws, Mary Ann. *Robert Motherwell With Pen and Brush.* London: Reaktion Books Ltd, 2003.

Fein, John M. *Toward Octavio Paz: A Reading of His Major Poems 1957–1976.* Lexington: The University Press of Kentucky, 1986.

Foster, David, ed. *Octavio Paz.* Boston: G.K. Hall & Co., 1986.

Terenzio, Stephanie. *The Prints of Robert Motherwell.* New York: Hudson Hills Press, 1991.

Weinberger, Eliot, ed. *Octavio Paz: The Collected Poems 1957–1987.* Manchester: Carcanet Press, 1988.

Born in a small town outside Mexico City in 1914, Octavio Paz is known for his modern poetry and prose. Early in his life, he learned the value of social causes from his father, a lawyer who took part in the Mexican Revolution. Paz studied both literature and law at the University of Mexico, but he left before earning a degree. His first book of poems, *Luna Silvestre* (Savage Moon), was published when he was only nineteen years old. After entering the Mexican diplomatic service, Paz lived in Paris during the late 1940s, where he befriended Albert Camus, André Breton and the Surrealists. He was also influenced by Chilean poet Pablo Neruda and Argentinean writer Jorge Luis Borges. In 1971 Paz returned to Mexico after teaching at numerous American universities, including Harvard, where he earned an honorary degree. In 1990 he was awarded the Nobel Prize for literature.

Published by the Limited Editions Club, *Three Poems* is a collaboration between Octavio Paz and abstract expressionist artist Robert Motherwell. The three poems that make up the book were originally published in a collection of Paz's poems from 1969 to 1975 entitled *Vuelta* (*Return*). The first poem is "Nocturno de San Ildefonso," or "San Ildefonso Nocturne." It reflects on Paz's younger days and is a shortened version of the original poem. The second poem, also called "Vuelta," is dedicated to José Alvarado. This return describes Paz's journey home to his birthplace, Mixcoac. The third poem, "The Skin of the World, The Sound of the World," was written for Motherwell and refers to various paintings and collages by the artist.

Motherwell was born in 1915 and had a relatively privileged upbringing in California. He attended Stanford University in 1932 where he studied literature, among other subjects. In 1940 he moved to New York and studied art history. It was there that he met André Breton and other Surrealists and became interested in the notion of "automatic" writing and drawing. He eventually became one of the leaders of the New York Abstract Expressionist Movement. In his writings and paintings, Motherwell drew from French Symbolists and Spanish and Mexican poets, including his friend Octavio Paz. He was also influenced by other European writers such as Rainer Maria Rilke and James Joyce as well as Zen philosophy and Oriental calligraphy.

According to Motherwell, the lithographs for *Three Poems* are not illustrations but images that emotionally connect with the subject matter. Eight of the nine prints, including the *Red Samurai* pictured here, were originally drawings for a 1967 project at the Museum of Modern Art in New York City. The remaining lithographs were done between 1986 and 1988 and were printed from one or two aluminum plates. The prints reflect the artist's Abstract Expressionist interest in autobiographical gesture and calligraphic marks.

SW

CATALOGUE 49
Walasse Ting
(b. 1929)
1¢ Life, 1964
(Dust jacket, pictured)
Printed text with lithographs,
serigraphs and photomechanical
prints
Museum of Art and Archaeology
University of Missouri-Columbia
94.8 c

MEASUREMENTS
41 x 58 centimeters
(Individual folios when opened)

REFERENCES
Arkus, Leon Anthony.
Fresh air school; exhibition of
paintings, 1972/73: Sam Francis,
Joan Mitchell, Walasse Ting.
Pittsburgh: Carnegie Institute
Museum of Art, 1972.

Ting, Walasse. "Near 1¢ Life."
ARTnews 65, no. 3 (May 1966):
38–39, 67–68.

—— , *1¢ Life*. Bern,
Switzerland: E.W. Kornfeld,
1964.

Wake Forest University,
Department of Art, Print
Collection, "PC 148, Walasse
Ting,"http://www.wfu.edu/
academics/art/pc/pc-ting.
html, 2006.

The 1964 book *1¢ Life* illustrated poems by Chinese-born artist Walasse Ting with original prints by twenty-seven different twentieth-century artists. Ting, born in Shanghai in 1929, studied at the Shanghai Art Academy. In 1950 he left China for Paris, where he was exposed to the art of Matisse and Picasso. The work of these artists left a powerful impression on Ting, whose depictions of women, birds, flowers and animals are known for their freshness, vivacity and dazzling color.

Ting moved to New York in 1958 at the peak of the Abstract Expressionist Movement. There, he befriended Sam Francis, an abstract expressionist who later helped produce *1¢ Life*. This was a project that realized Ting's quest to produce a book as "exciting as Times Square, color bright as neon light, hot as expresso . . . like hundred flower garden."

Ting began writing poems for *1¢ Life* in 1961. After completing the poems, the author described himself as having "61 poems, no money to publish, just dream, day and night, angel come to publish book" (Ting, *ARTnews*, 39). Sam Francis and Eli Kornfeld provided Ting with the means to publish the book. They reportedly said, "We are not angels, but we are going to publish the book, even if we go to jail, it is O.K.!" (Ting, *ARTnews*, 67). Francis gave Ting the money to purchase the more than seventeen tons of paper he used to produce the project while Kornfeld provided printing equipment. Twenty-seven artists who were friends and acquaintances of Ting, many with contrasting tastes and styles, contributed original lithographs to illustrate the poems. The artists include: Pierre Alechinsky, Alfred Leslie, Robert Indiana, Karel Appel, Andy Warhol, Robert Rauschenberg, Roy Lichtenstein, Tom Wesselmann and Claes Oldenburg. According to Ting, it was not exactly a smooth process. He said, "Four printing companies work one year, everything must be perfect, changes and reprintings, money running away like April rain in Paris" (Ting, *ARTnews*, 67).

Two thousand regular edition, numbered copies of the book were printed in France along with 100 special edition copies that were printed on handmade paper, numbered and signed by the artists. Of these 100 copies, forty were reserved for the artists and collaborators, twenty reserved for New York, twenty reserved for Paris and twenty for the rest of the world. The Museum of Art and Archaeology owns copy 1950/2000 from the large edition. The dust jacket, pictured on the facing page, represents a stylized and over-painted photo of Ting.

In his attempt to merge Eastern and Western influences, Ting's poems describe elements of Western pop culture while imitating the sound of his native Chinese language. This reflects his belief that "[Chinese] artists are, to a certain extent, schizophrenics," and that they "try to resolve the contradiction by conscious means, by using traditional Chinese art in an attempt to modernize Chinese painting" (Wake Forest University, 2). *1¢ Life* is a striking amalgamation of Abstract Expressionism and pop art. Leon Anthony Arkus of the Carnegie Institute Museum of Art commented that, "Walasse Ting speaks and writes of his art in a continuous stream of poetic images. And just as his canvases are large poems, his poetry summons forth to our inner eye his paintings—glowing with color and sensuality" (Arkus, 2). The stunning combination of lithographs from a number of iconic artists of the 1960s leaves the viewer with the impression that, in a society in which the amount of one's wealth can determine that person's happiness, even a one-cent life can still be exciting.

HR

cover design by michael upton

CATALOGUE 50
Claes Oldenburg
(American, b. 1929)
"All Kinds of Love"
*From Walasse Ting's **1¢ Life**, 1964*
(Page numbers 136 & 137, pictured)
Color lithograph
Museum of Art and Archaeology
University of Missouri-Columbia
94.8 a

MEASUREMENTS
41 x 58 centimeters
(Individual folios when opened)

CATALOGUE 51
Tom Wesselmann
(American, 1931-2004)
"Sun in Stomach . . ."
*From Walasse Ting's **1¢ Life**, 1964*
(Page numbers 64 & 65, pictured)
Color lithograph
Museum of Art and Archaeology
University of Missouri-Columbia
94.8 a

MEASUREMENTS
41 x 58 centimeters
(Individual folios when opened)

ALL KINDS OF LOVE

Two selections from Walasse Ting's *1¢ Life* are featured in this exhibition and catalogue. Both are examples of pop art that made statements about consumption in the 1960s. Throughout *1¢ Life*, there are many references to food and eating. This theme is reflected in *All Kinds of Love*, two companion lithographs by Claes Oldenburg. The prints depict the profile of a woman opposite a slice of cake. The layers of the woman's hair mirror the layers of the cake, which establishes a parallel between the woman and cake as consumable commodities. Commenting on Oldenburg, Ting writes in the text of *1¢ Life*, "Master of drawing, said Alechinsky. I think his line like fish, his hand like fishtail."

In *Sun in Stomach . . .*, Tom Wesselmann presents another image of food. Like other pop artists, he combined the traditional concept of still life with an interest in depicting images and objects from popular culture, particularly food and its packaging. By using colors and graphic techniques associated with advertising, Wesselmann created a visual commentary on the production and consumption of both art and the household goods depicted in his works.

HR

REFERENCES
Ting, Walasse Ting. "Near 1¢
Life." *ARTnews* 65, no. 3 (May
1966): 38-39, 67-68.

———, *1¢ Life*. Bern,
Switzerland: E.W. Kornfeld,
1964.

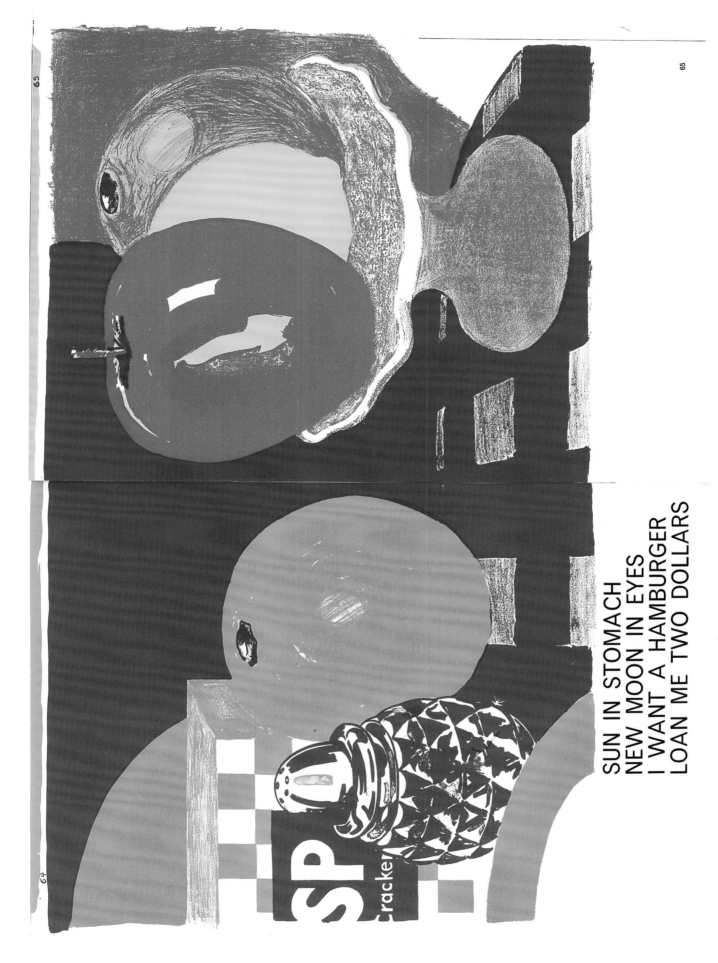

SUN IN STOMACH
NEW MOON IN EYES
I WANT A HAMBURGER
LOAN ME TWO DOLLARS

CATALOGUE 52
Margaret Kaufman
(American, b. 1941)
Deep in the Territory, *ca. 1999.*
(Leaf corresponding to the book's
tenth poem "Nell's Quilt,"
pictured)
Illustrated by Clare Van Vliet and
Audrey Holden
Mixed media and printed text
Special Collections, Ellis Library
University of Missouri-Columbia

MEASUREMENTS
21 x 23 centimeters (cover)

Margaret Kaufman is a poet, fiction writer, editor and teacher. A graduate of the Warren Wilson MFA Program for Writers, she currently edits fiction for *The Marlboro Review*, a journal of contemporary fiction, poetry, translations and essays. Kaufman is one of the founding members of the Sixteen Rivers Press, a shared-work, nonprofit poetry collective that provides alternative publishing avenues for San Francisco Bay Area poets. In 2002 the Sixteen Rivers Press published Kaufman's first full collection of poetry, *Snake at the Wrist*. Today, Kaufman leads writing workshops and continues to write short fiction in Kentfield, California.

Deep in the Territory is one of several letterpress editions of Kaufman's poems issued by Janus Press. The poems for *Deep in the Territory* were inspired by Plainswomen and their quilts, and just as quilts have traditionally been made collaboratively, the creation of this handmade book was made possible by a partnership of women. After reading the poems and wanting to work with Kaufman, Claire Van Vliet, founder of Janus Press, designed the structure of the book. The collage illustrations were cut and assembled by Audrey Holden, and the clamshell box that houses the book was made by Judi Conant and Mary Richardson in Maidstone, Vermont.

The structure of the book also relates to the way quilts are pieced together and quilted. The book's "quilted" paper leaves are made up of shapes that are not glued in place but instead are held together in interlocking and woven patterns. The quilted pages were made with a variety of handmade papers such as Cal-ling, Cave Paper, black kozo and Japanese Chiyogami.

The poems for *Deep in the Territory* were written with particular quilts and quilt forms in mind. The poem, *"Nell's Quilt,"* and its illustration relate to "crazy quilts." Crazy quilts present seemingly random patterns organized with studied artfulness. Kaufman describes them as such:

> *That sort of quilt was frequently done with finer fabrics than not: velvet, satin, brocade—and was an occasion for the quilter to show off her fine stitchery with a variety of stitches used to connect one piece of fabric to another, sometimes to appliqué, sometimes to embroider a bouquet or an object like an owl or a teapot—things with some significance to the maker, or perhaps just something that caught her fancy or for which she had a kit or magazine template . . . For me, the original sense of craze, the thing you see beneath the surface, reminded me of my mother's smile, her delicately wrinkled face, the way her smile made all the surfaces readjust themselves. There's no one smile, no one pattern for a crazy quilt. An abundance.*
> (Kaufman, letter to the author)

Using the poems as their inspiration, Van Vliet and Holden created the woven patterns to reflect the text and relate to fabric quilting. Included in the clamshell box is a plastic bag of paper scraps leftovers from the creation of the book. These paper fragments relate to the fabric scraps that make up quilts.

SW

REFERENCES
Van Vliet, Claire, and
Elizabeth Steiner. *Woven and*
Interlocking Book Structures:
from the Janus, Steiner and Fefn
Presses. Neware, Vt.: Janus
Gefn Unlimited, 2002.

CATALOGUE 53
Luis Borges
(Argentinean, 1899–1986) and
Heather Weston
(American, b. 1966)
"Borges and I," 2001
Printed and embossed text
Special Collections, Ellis Library
University of Missouri-Columbia

MEASUREMENTS
11 x 11 centimeters (cover)

Before receiving her master's degree in Book Arts from Camberwell College in London, Heather Weston worked in the fields of psychotherapy and psychiatry. Many of her books deal with psychological territory such as the experience of schizophrenia, alcoholism, suicide and codependence in parent-child relationships. She draws a parallel between the structure of the mind and the structure of books. When she began making books, she found that the process helped to inform her own understanding of certain psychological realities.

The text of *Borges and I* consists of an English translation of a short piece of prose by Argentinean modernist writer Jorges Luis Borges. Borges is known for his writings that explore metaphysics, language and the nature of identity. This translation of the essay *Borges and I* was first published in the 1964 book *Labyrinths*, a collection of Borges' stories, writings and poems.

In *Borges and I* the author describes an internal battle between Borges the man and Borges the writer. He uses both first and third person in an attempt to negotiate the balance of his personal self and his public self. His claim that, "I am destined to perish, definitively, and only some instant of myself can survive in him," refutes the idea that an author continues to exist indefinitely through the fame of his writing. Instead, Borges believes that only a small part of the real Borges will survive in the Borges persona.

Heather Weston reproduced the entire text of *Borges and I* in her accordion-formatted book. By printing the offset text on black paper and blind embossing certain words and letters, she created a subtext for the essay. On one level, the color of the book and text allude to the fact that Borges went blind in 1955 at the age of fifty-six. In the blind-embossed text, Weston created another narrative within that of Borges' that reads:

> *I map in vain our hostile relationship; I got on living just to confess that those pages cannot save what is good, not even language. Besides, I am definitively and only of myself, I am everything, I am falsifying and magnifying, I long to persist in being; eternally to be a stone and tiger. I shall remain myself (if it is true that I am someone), I recognise myself in many others. Years ago I tried to free myself and went from the mythologies of the suburbs to the games with time and infinity; I shall have to imagine other things. Thus my life is a flight and I lose everything and everything belongs to oblivion.*

This text interrupts the flow of the original Borges soliloquy and plays on the conflict of the id and ego. If the viewer holds the book at different angles, he or she can highlight the original Borges text or the raised text. The constant play between the two kinds of type also reflects the conflict between the two Borgeses. In the text, the author describes how his personal self melded with his public self, "Little by little, I am giving over everything to him."

SW

REFERENCES
MacAdam, Alfred J. "Origins and Narratives." *MLN* (2) vol. 95, Hispanic issue (March 1980): 424–435.

Maurois, André. "Preface," in *Labyrinths: Selected Stories and Other Writings*. Edited by Donald A. Yates and James E. Irby. New York: New Directions Publishing Corporation, 1964.

Weston, Heather. Interview by Vicky Stewart. Vamp & Tramp Booksellers, LLC, May 2004.

Nancy Morejón is one of Cuba's foremost contemporary poets. Of Spanish, Chinese and African descent, she focuses on the post-colonial Caribbean experience in her work. In 2001 she won Cuba's national prize for literature, and in 2006 the XV International Book Fair of Cuba was dedicated to her work.

Ana Mendieta is Morejón's poetic elegy to Ana Mendieta (1948–1985), one of the greatest Cuban artists of the twentieth century. Mendieta left her homeland in 1961, at the age of twelve, as part of the Peter Pan Operation. During this venture, several U.S. based organizations convinced parents in Cuba to transport 14,000 children to the U.S. without their families. Mendieta spent her teen years in an Iowa orphanage and various foster homes. She studied art at the University of Iowa, and as a mature artist, became known for her performance art, body art, earth works and site-specific installations. Among her most famous creations are her "silueta," or "silhouettes," in which she imprinted her body into the earth, water and flora of the landscape. These ephemeral productions were documented

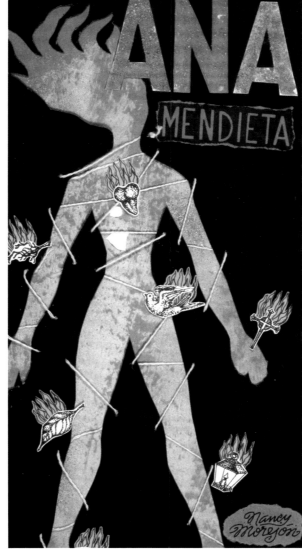

CATALOGUE 54
Nancy Morejón
(Cuban, b. 1944) and
Rolando Estévez
(Cuban, b. 1953)
Ana Mendieta, *2003*
(**Cover**, *pictured*)
Mixed media and printed text on paper
Published by Vigía.
Lent by Dr. Juanamaria Cordones Cook

MEASUREMENTS
39.7 x 20 centimeters

in haunting photographs that show the outline of Mendieta's body in mud, flowers, scorched earth and other materials. In the 1980s she married minimalist artist Carl Andre, and it was from their shared apartment that she fell to her death in 1985 at the age of thirty-six. Although Andre was tried and found not guilty of Mendieta's murder, her death is still viewed through a cloud of controversy and suspicion.

In 2003 Nancy Morejon collaborated with the publishing collective Ediciones Vigía to produce this book. Ediciones Vigía was founded in 1985 in the Cuban city of Matanzas, east of Havana. It brings together illustrators, designers, poets and writers to produce limited-edition, hand-constructed books of poetry and literature. The collective incorporates recycled and natural materials into its editions, each of which is limited to 200 hand-signed and numbered copies. The publishers combine inexpensive popular printing methods with sophisticated craftsmanship. The texts and some images are printed using photocopiers and mimeograph machines while the books themselves are constructed, colored and bound by hand. Many incorporate collage and moving parts into their design. On the cover of *Ana Mendieta*, the silhouette cut out of paper recalls the artist's silueta artwork, and the mixture of various materials makes reference to her experimental creations.

JS

REFERENCES
Alegria, Maria Eugenia, Rolando Estevez, and Alfredo Zaldivar. "Vigía: The endless publications of Matanzas," in *Bridges to Cuba*. Edited by Ruth Behar. Ann Arbor, Mich.: University of Michigan Press, 1995, 316-322.

Cothern, Lynn. "Art of the book at Ediciones Vigía in Matanzas, Cuba." *SALALM Newsletter* 26, no. 6 (1999): 166–168.

Viso, Olga. *Ana Mendieta: Earth Body; Sculpture and Performance, 1972–1985*. Ostfilderne-Ruit: Hatje Cantz Publishers, 2004. An exhibition catalogue.

BIBLIOGRAPHY

Adler, Elmer.
  "The Making of a Book." *The Dolphin* 2 (1935):144–153.
Alegria, Maria Eugenia, Rolando Estevez, and Alfredo Zaldivar.
  "Vigía: The endless publications of Matanzas," in *Bridges to Cuba.* Edited by Ruth Behar. Ann Arbor, Mich.: University of Michigan Press, 1995, 316-322.
Alexander, Christine A.
  A Bibliography of the Manuscripts of Charlotte Brontë. Westport, Conn.: Meckler Publishing and the Brontë Society, 1982.
  ——— . *The Early Writings of Charlotte Brontë.* New York: Prometheus, 1983.
  ——— , ed. *An Edition of the Early Writings of Charlotte Brontë.* Vol. II, part 1. Oxford: Shakespeare Head Press, 1991, 269–315.
  ——— , and Margaret Smith. *The Oxford Companion to the Brontës.* Oxford: Oxford University Press, 2003.
"An Account of the Micrographia, or the Physiological Description of Minute Bodies, made by Magnifying Glasses." *Philosophical Transactions* 1, no. 2 (1665): 27–32.
Andrade, E. N. da C.
  "Robert Hooke, F. R. S. (1635–1703)." *Notes and Records of the Royal Society of London* 15 (July 1960): 137–145.
Archer, Mildred.
  Early Views of India: The Picturesque Journeys of Thomas and William Daniell, 1786–1794; The Complete Aquatints. New York: Thames and Hudson, 1980.
Arkus, Leon Anthony.
  Fresh air school; exhibition of paintings, 1972/73: Sam Francis, Joan Mitchell, Walasse Ting. Pittsburgh: Carnegie Institute Museum of Art, 1972.
Arts and Crafts Essays. London: Rivington, Percival, & Company, 1893. Reprint, 1996.
Audubon, John James.
  Audubon and His Journals, with Zoological and Other Notes by Elliott Coues. Ed. Maria Audubon, 2 vols. New York: Charles Scribner's Sons, 1897. Reprint, New York: Dover Publications, 1994.
  ——— . *Audubon's Mammals: The Quadrupeds of America Complete and Unabridged.* Secaucus, N.J.: Wellfleet Press, 2005.
Barker, Juliet.
  The Brontës. New York: St. Martin's Press, 1994.
Barratt, Carrie Rebora.
  The Art of Henry Inman. Washington, D.C.: Smithsonian Institution, 1987. An exhibition catalogue.
Bass, Ruth.
  "Matchmakers." *ArtNews* (February, 1987): 9–10.
Batey, Mavis.
  "The Picturesque: An Overview." *The Picturesque* 22, no. 2 (winter 1994): 121–32.
Benton, Megan.
  Beauty and the Book: Fine Editions and Cultural Distinction in America. New Haven: Yale University Press, 2000.
Benton, Thomas Hart.
  An Artist in America, 4th ed. Columbia, Missouri: University of Missouri Press, 1983.
Beronä, David.
  "Picture Stories: Erick Drooker and the Tradition of Woodcut Novels." *Print Quarterly* 20, no. 1 (March 2003): 61–73.
Bindman, David.
  Blake as an Artist. Oxford: E. P. Dutton; Phaidon, 1977.
Biographical Dictionary of Indians of the Americas. 2 vols. Newport Beach, CA: American Indian Publishers Inc, 1991.
Boehme, Sarah.
  "Omega: John James Audubon's Final Artistic Journey," in *John James Audubon in the West. The Last Expedition, Mammals of North America.* Edited by Sarah Boehme. New York: Harry N. Abrams Inc, 2000, 35–70. An exhibition catalogue.
Boehme, Sarah, ed.
  John James Audubon in the West. The Last Expedition, Mammals of North America. New York: Harry N. Abrams Inc, 2000. An exhibition catalogue.
Bolliger, Hans.
  "Introduction," in *Picasso's Vollard Suite.* Translated by Norbert Guterman. New York: Harry N. Abrams Inc, 1997.
Bowers, Shirley H.
  "Captured on Canvas: McKenney-Hall's *History of the Indian Tribes of North America.*" *Florida Historical Quarterly* 71 (1993), 339–347.
Brontë, Charlotte.
  The Secret and Lily Hart: Two Tales. Edited and transcribed by William Holz. Columbia: University of Missouri Press, 1978.
Buchanan, Handasyde.
  Thornton's Temple of Flora. London: George Rainbird Limited, 1951.
Caine, William Sproston.
  Picturesque India: A Handbook for European Travelers; Illustrations Drawn by John Pedder, H. Sheppard Dale, and H.H. Stanton. London: G. Routledge, 1890. Reprint, 1982.
Carter, John, and Percy H. Muir.
  Printing and the Mind of Man. Munich: K. Pressler, 1983.
Caws, Mary Ann.
  Robert Motherwell With Pen and Brush. London: Reaktion Books Ltd, 2003.
Christian, Mildred G.
  "A Census of Brontë Manuscripts in the United States: Part One." *Trollopian* 2, no. 3 (Dec. 1947): 190.
Collester, Jeanne Colette.
  Frederick Oakes Sylvester: The Principia Collection. St. Louis: Principia Corp., 1988.

Cosentino, Andrew.
  The Paintings of Charles Bird King (1785–1862). Washington, D.C.: Smithsonian Institution Press for the National Collection of Fine Arts, 1977.
Cothern, Lynn.
  "Art of the book at Ediciones Vigía in Matanzas, Cuba." *SALALM Newsletter* 26, no. 6 (1999): 166–168.
Crouther, Betty J.
  "Deciphering the Mississippi River Iconography of Frederick Oakes Sylvester," *Muse* 20 (1986): 81–89.
Crump, R. W.
  Charlotte and Emily Brontë, 1846–1915: A Reference Guide. Boston: G. K. Hall, 1982.
Damon, S. Foster.
  Blake's Job: William Blake's Illustrations of the Book of Job. Providence, Rhode Island: Brown University Press, 1966.
de Hamel, Christopher.
  The British Library Guide to Manuscript Illumination: History and Techniques. London: University of Toronto Press, 2001.
Desmarais, Jane Haville.
  The Beardsley Industry: The Critical Reception in England and France 1893–1914. Aldershot: Ashgate Press, 1998.
Desmond, Ray.
  Great Natural History Books and their Creators. London: British Library, 2003.
Dibner, Bern.
  Heralds of Science as Represented by Two Hundred Epochal Books Selected from the Burndy Library. Norwalk, Conn.: Burndy Library, 1955.
Dobell, Clifford.
  Anthony van Leeuwenhoek and His "Little Animals." New York: Harcourt, 1932.
Duff, Hart Davis.
  Audubon's Elephant: America's Greatest Naturalists and the Making of "Birds of America." New York: H. Holt, 2004.
Eaves, Morris, ed.
  The Cambridge Companion Guide to William Blake. Cambridge: Cambridge University Press, 2003.
Eddy, Linda R.
  "Achilles Contending with the Rivers: Flaxman Translates Homer." *The Stanford Museum*, 6–7 (1976–1977): 10–17.
Fara, Patricia.
  Newton: The Making of Genius. New York: Columbia University Press, 2002.
Fein, John M.
  Toward Octavio Paz: A Reading of His Major Poems 1957–1976. Lexington: The University Press of Kentucky, 1986.
Ficacci, Luigi.
  Piranesi: The Complete Etchings. London: Taschen, 2000.
Fletcher, Ian.
  Aubrey Beardsley. Boston: Twayne Publishers, 1987.
Florman, Lisa.
  Myth and Metamorphosis: Picasso's Classical Prints from the 1930s. Cambridge, Mass: The MIT Press, 2000.
Ford, Brian J.
  Single Lens: The Story of the Simple Microscope. New York: Harper and Row, 1985.
Foster, David, ed.
  Octavio Paz. Boston: G.K. Hall & Co., 1986.
Friedman, Winifred.
  Boydell's Shakespeare Gallery. New York and London: Garland Publishing Inc, 1976.
Fries, Waldemar H.
  The Double Elephant Folio: The Story of Audubon's "Birds of America." Chicago: American Library Association, 1973.
Goethe, Johann Wolfgang von.
  Conversations with Eckerman. Translated by John Oxenford. London: 1850. Reprint, San Francisco: North Point Press, 1984.
Gottfried, Sello.
  Grandville. Das gesamte Werk. 2 vols. Berlin: Henschelveri, 1970.
Grandville, J. J., and Taxile Delord.
  The Flowers Personified. Translated by N. Cleaveland. New York: R. Martin, 1847.
Gray, George J.
  A bibliography of the works of Sir Isaac Newton, together with a list of books illustrating his works; with notes by George J. Gray. Cambridge: Bowes and Bowes, 1907.
Gross, Anthony.
  Etching, Engraving, and Intaglio Printing. London: Oxford University Press, 1973.
Guillaud, Jacqueline, and Maurice Guillaud.
  Matisse: Rhythm and Line. Paris: Guillaud Editions, 1987.
Hamlyn, Robin.
  "The Shakespeare Galleries of John Boydell and James Woodmason," in *Shakespeare in Art*. Edited by Jane Martineau. London and New York: Merell Publishers, 2003, 97–101. An exhibition catalogue.
Hargreaves, G. D.
  "The Publishing of *Poems* by Currer, Ellis and Acton Bell." *Brontë Society Transactions* 15 (1969): 294–300.
Harris, Eileen, and Nicholas Savage.
  "Stuart and Revett," in *British Architectural Books and Writers (1556–1785)*. Cambridge: Cambridge University Press, 1990, 439–450.
Hindman, Sarah, and Nina Rowe, eds.
  Manuscript Illumination in the Modern Ages: Recovery and Reconstruction. Evanston, Ill.: Mary and Leigh Block Museum of Art, 2001.
Horan, James David.
  The McKenney-Hall Portrait Gallery of American Indians. New York: Bramhall House, 1986.
Houfe, Simon.
  The Dictionary of 19th Century British Book Illustrators. Suffolk: Antique Collector's Club Ltd., 1998.

Hyams, Edward.
    Capability Brown and Humphry Repton. London: Dent, 1971.
Jobert, Barthélémy, ed.
    Delacroix: Le trait romantique. Paris: Bibliothèque nationale de France, 1998. An exhibition catalogue.
Johnson, Deborah.
    Old Master Drawings from the Museum of Art, Rhode Island School of Design. Providence, R. I.: Rhode Island School of Design, 1983.
Jones, Dan Burne.
    "Books Illustrated by Rockwell Kent." *American Book Collector* 14 (1964): 43–50.
Kammen, Michael.
    The Lively Arts: Gilbert Seldes and the Transformation of Cultural Criticism in the United States. Oxford: Oxford University Press, 1996.
Keynes, Geoffrey.
    A Bibliography of Dr. Robert Hooke. Oxford: Clarendon Press, 1960.
King, James.
    William Blake: His Life. New York: St. Martin's Press, 1991.
Klonk, Charlotte.
    Science and the Perception of Nature: British Landscape Art in the Late Eighteenth and Early Nineteenth Centuries. New Haven; London: Yale University Press, 1996.
Le Roy, Julien-David.
    The Ruins of the Most Beautiful Monuments of Greece. "Introduction" by Robin Middleton. Translated by David Britt. Los Angeles: Getty
      Publications, 2004.
Leask, Negel.
    Curiosity and the Aesthetics of Travel Writing, 1770–1840: 'From an Antique Land.' Oxford: Oxford University Press, 2002.
Lennox-Boyd, Christopher.
    "The Prints Themselves: Production, Marketing, and their Survival," in *Boydell's Shakespeare Gallery*. Edited by Walter Pape and Frederick
      Burwick. Essen and Bottrop: Peter Pomp, 1996, 45–53.
McCausland, Elizabeth, ed.
    Work for Artists: What? Where? How? New York: American Artists Group Inc, 1947.
MacAdam, Alfred J.
    "Origins and Narratives." *MLN* (2) vol. 95, Hispanic issue (March 1980): 424–435.
Macfall, Haldane.
    Aubrey Beardsley: The Man and His Work. London: John Lane The Bodley Head Limited, 1928.
Marqusee, Michael.
    "Introduction," in *Faust with Eighteen Lithographs by Eugène Delacroix*. New York: Paddington Press, 1977.
Mathews, John Joseph.
    The Osages: Children of the Middle Waters. Norman: University of Oklahoma Press, 1982.
Maurois, André.
    "Preface," in *Labyrinths: Selected Stories and Other Writings*. Edited by Donald A. Yates and James E. Irby. New York: New Directions
      Publishing Corporation, 1964.
Mountnorris, George Annesley.
    Voyages and Travels in India, Ceylon, the Red Sea, Abyssinia and Egypt in the Years 1802, 1803, 1804, 1805, and 1806. 3 vols. London: William
      Miller, 1809.
Naylor, Gillian.
    The Arts and Crafts Movement. London: Sudio Vista Publishers, 1971.
Newman, Ralph Geoffrey.
    Great and Good Books: A Bibliographical Catalogue of the Limited Editions Club, 1929-1985. Chicago: Ralph Geoffrey Newman Inc, 1989.
Newton, Sir Isaac.
    The Principia mathematical principles of natural philosophy; a new translation by I. Bernard Cohen and Anne Whitman assisted by Julia Budenz;
      preceded by A guide to Newton's Principia by I. Bernard Cohen. Berkeley, Calif.: University of California Press, ca. 1999.
Palm, L. C.
    "Leeuwenhoek and Other Dutch Correspondents of the Royal Society." *Notes and Records of the Royal Society of London* 43, no. 2 (July 1989):
      191–207.
Pape, Walter, and Frederick Burwick, eds.
    Boydell's Shakespeare Gallery. Essen and Bottrop: Peter Pomp, 1996.
Parker, G. H.
    "Anthony Van Leeuwenhoek and His Microscopes." *Scientific Monthly* 37, no. 5 (Nov. 1933): 434–441.
Passel, Anne.
    Charlotte and Emily Brontë: An Annotated Bibliography. New York: Garland, 1979.
"Peggy Bacon, Kindly Humorist, Has a Show." *The Art Digest* 8 (March 1, 1934): 8.
"Peggy Bacon–Who Laughs at Life." *The Art Digest* 11, 12 (May 1, 1937): 9.
Peterson, William.
    A Bibliography of the Kelmscott Press. Oxford: Clarendon Press, 1984.
Raine, Kathleen.
    The Human Face of God: William Blake and the Book of Job. New York: Thames and Hudson, 1982.
Ratchford, Fannie.
    Legends of Angria: Compiled from the Early Writings of Charlotte Brontë. New Haven: Yale University Press, 1933.
  —— . *The Brontës' Web of Childhood*. New York: Russell & Russell, 1964.
Ray, Gordon.
    The Art of the French Illustrated Book 1700 to 1914. 2 vols. New York: The Pierpont Morgan Library and Cornell University Press, 1982.
Repton, Humphry.
    The Red Books of Humphry Repton. London: Basilisk Press, 1976.
Review of *Philosophiae naturalis principia mathematica*. *Philosophical Transactions of the Royal Society* 16 (1686): 297.

Rhodes, Richard.
    John James Audubon: The Making of an American. New York: Vintage Books, 2006.
Robinson, Tom.
    Buttons. New York: The Viking Press, 1938. Reprint, 1966.
Schierbeek, Abraham.
    Measuring the Invisible World: The Life and Works of Antoni van Leeuwenhoek. New York: Abelard-Schumann, 1959.
Scott, Jonathan.
    Piranesi. New York: St. Martin's Press, 1975.
Sérullaz, Arlette.
    "Un parcours initiatique. Delacroix illustrateur de *Faust*," in *Faust*. Edited by Diane de Selliers. Paris: Diane de Selliers, 1997, 11–20.
Sitwell, Sacheverell, and Wilfrid Blunt.
    Great Flower Books, 1700-1900: A Bibliographic Record of Two Centuries of Finely-Illustrated Flower Books. London: Collins, 1956.
Slatkin, Carole Anne.
    "Little Blue Heron," in *John James Audubon: The Watercolors for "The Birds of America."* Edited by Annette Blaugrund and Theodore E. Stebbins, Jr. New York: Villard books, Random House, 1993, 195–197.
Souder, William.
    Under a Wild Sky: John James Audubon and the Making of "The Birds of America." New York: North Point Press, 2004.
Stein, John Bethune.
    "On the Trail of Van Leeuwenhoek." *Scientific Monthly* 32, no. 2 (Feb. 1931): 116–134.
Steiner, Bill.
    Audubon Art Prints: A Collector's Guide to Every Early Edition. Columbia, S.C.: University of South Carolina Press, 2003.
Stroud, Dorothy.
    Humphry Repton. London: Country Life, 1962.
Sturgis, Matthew.
    Aubrey Beardsley, A Biography. London: HarperCollins Publishers, 1998.
Tarbell, Roberta.
    Peggy Bacon: Personalities and Places. Washington, D.C.: National Collection of Fine Arts, Smithsonian Institution Press, 1975.
Terenzio, Stephanie.
    The Prints of Robert Motherwell. New York: Hudson Hills Press, 1991.
Thomas Hart Benton's Illustrations from Mark Twain: The Adventures of Tom Sawyer, The Adventures of Huckleberry Finn, and Life on the Mississippi from the State from The State Historical Society of Missouri Collection. Columbia, Missouri: Mid-America Arts Alliance, 1976.
Thompson, Susan Otis.
    American Book Design and William Morris. London: Oak Knoll Press and The British Library, 1977. Reprint, 1996.
Thornton, Robert.
    The Temple of Flora. London: 1799–1807. Reprint, Boston: New York Graphic Society, 1981.
Ting, Walasse.
    "Near 1¢ Life." *ARTnews* 65, no. 3 (May 1966): 38–39, 67–68.
——— . *1¢ Life*. Bern, Switzerland: E.W. Kornfeld, 1964.
Tucker, Nicholas.
    The Child and the Book: A Psychological and Literary Exploration. London: Cambridge University Press, 1981.
Turner, Caroline, and Roger Benjamin.
    Matisse. Australia: Queensland Art Gallery, 1995.
Twain, Mark.
    The Adventures of Huckleberry Finn. Illustrated by Thomas Hart Benton. New York: The Limited Editions Club, 1942.
Tyler, Ron.
    Audubon's Great National Work: The Royal Octavo Edition of "The Birds of America." Austin: University of Texas Press, 1993.
——— . "The Publication of *The Viviparous Quadrupeds of North America*," in *John James Audubon in the West. The Last Expeditions, Mammals of North America*. Edited by Sarah Boehme. New York: Harry N. Abrams, Inc., 2000, 119–182. An exhibition catalogue.
Van Vliet, Claire, and Elizabeth Steiner.
    Woven and Interlocking Book Structures: from the Janus, Steiner and Fefn Presses. Neware, VT: Janus Gefn Unlimited, 2002.
Vaughan, William.
    William Blake. Princeton, New Jersey: Princeton University Press, 1999.
Viola, Herman.
    The Indian Legacy of Charles Bird King. Washington, D. C.: Smithsonian Institution, 1976.
——— . *Thomas L. McKenney: Architect of America's Early Indian Policy, 1816-1830*. Chicago: Sage Books, 1974.
Viso, Olga.
    Ana Mendieta: Earth Body; Sculpture and Performance, 1972–1985. Ostfilderne-Ruit: Hatje Cantz Publishers, 2004. An exhibition catalogue.
Wake Forest University, Department of Art, Print Collection, http://www.wfu.edu/academics/art/pc/pc-ting.html
Ward, Geoffrey C., and Dayton Duncan.
    Mark Twain. New York: Alfred A. Knopf, 2001.
Ward, Lynd.
    Storyteller without Words: The Wood Engravings of Lynd Ward. New York: Harry N. Abrams Inc, 1974.
Weinberger, Eliot, ed.
    Octavio Paz: The Collected Poems 1957–1987. Manchester: Carcanet Press, 1988.
Weinglass, David H.
    Prints and Engraved Illustrations By and After Henry Fuseli. Aldershot: Scolar Press, 1994.
Weston, Heather.
    Interview by Vicky Stewart. Vamp & Tramp Booksellers, LLC, May 2004.
Whinney, Margaret.
    "Flaxman and the Eighteenth Century," *Journal of the Warburg Courtauld Institute* 19 (1956): 269–282.

Wick, Peter A.
    "Introduction," in *Les Fleurs animées: The Engraved Illustrations of J. J. Grandville*. New York: George Braziller, 1981.
Wiebenson, Dora.
    Sources of Greek Revival Architecture. London: A. Zwemmer, 1969.
Willett, Perry.
    The Silent Shout: Frans Masereel, Lynd Ward, and the Novel in Woodcuts. Bloomington: Indiana University Libraries, 1997.
William Morris and the Art of the Book. Oxford: Oxford University Press; The Pierpont Morgan Library, 1976.
Williams, Paul O.
    Frederick Oakes Sylvester: the Artist's Encounter with Elsah. Elsah, Ill.: Historic Elsah Foundation, 1986.
Wilton-Ely, John.
    The Mind and Art of Giovanni Battista Piranesi. London: Thames and Hudson, 1978.